ON THE COVER: Abigail Washburn & the Sparrow Quartet at the Lake Superior Big Top Chautauqua in Washburn, Wisconsin, July 10, 2008. Photograph by Deone Jahnke, art direction by Béla Fleck, cover design by Grant Alden.
THE REST OF THE STORY: Béla Fleck pronounced the band's initial pose (above) BOR-RING! and repositioned them for what became the cover. He had, however, misplaced his white tie, so Casey Driessen took a sheet of white paper towel and carefully tore a tie-shape out of it. They taped the new "tie" under Fleck's collar and went on with the photo shoot.

Copyright © 2008 by the University of Texas Press
All rights reserved
Printed in the United States of America
First edition, 2008

Requests for permission to reproduce material from this work should be sent to:
    Permissions
    University of Texas Press
    P.o. Box 7819
    Austin, TX 78713-7819
    www.utexas.edu/utpress/about/bpermission.html

∞ The paper used in this book meets the minimum requirements of ANSI/NISO Z39.48-1992
(R1997) (Permanence of Paper).

ISBN 978-0-292-71928-6

Library of Congress Control Number: 2008931429

NO DEPRESSION

the bookazine (whatever that is) #76 • fall 2008

hello stranger

S IT TURNED out, the angels who interceded to preserve *No Depression* — responding to the publishers' note in the penultimate March-April 2008 edition of our magazine — were mostly well-known to us. Some who responded were rank strangers; all were generous and kind, as have been our friends, readers, and families.

But we should not have been surprised to find that the two key players in what *No Depression* will become arose from our small circle of friends. *ND* has always been first and foremost a community of cantankerous companions, joined together by an abiding fondness for extraordinary music, regardless of its commercial success.

Dave Hamrick, who had shepherded our tenth-anniversary compilation of articles through publication at the University of Texas Press (formally, *The Best Of No Depression: Writing About American Music,* and still for sale at better bookstores everywhere), spent long hours typing and thinking and talking to us about various solutions. We all ended up with the curious project you now hold: A bookazine.

A bookazine. This is one of those fusion things one reads about and maybe sees on the shelves, but what — exactly — such a thing is, we confess not to know. Nor to care, not really. Yes, there are models for this hybrid kind of magazine in book form, and we looked at several of them. But they weren't what we are,

or had been, or wanted to become, and the form seems hardly settled into any one particular notion. And so we ignored the ready models and plunged blindly forward.

Same way we started a magazine, thirteen years back.

As with the first years of the magazine, we sought to start this new venture simply (though, happily, with much higher production values!). It is our hope to play more loosely with the format of our new bookazine venture as we — and you — become more accustomed to its strengths and limitations.

We began, however, with certain clear understandings: In the age of the internet, some kinds of more time-sensitive content were ill-suited to a semi-annual publication. Which is where our second angel stepped forward. You know her, a bit, we hope, for Kyla Fairchild has been managing the circulation and advertising sales and many of the business affairs of *No Depression* almost since it began. On extremely short notice she has pulled together a team of experts to rebuild the *No Depression* website (that is: NoDepression.com), to adapt it to the ever-changing possibilities afforded by instant and interactive communication.

Which means that our live reviews will appear online rather than in these pages, as will the vast majority of record reviews. Old habits die hard, and so you'll find an appendix of sorts in this volume reviewing albums of particular prominence within our purview that were released during this edition's broader time-window. The website will offer other enticements, as well — including nearly all the contents of our 75 back-issues — and is set to relaunch at roughly the same time this first bookazine appears.

As for this first bookazine, then...one of

the ideas around which we began to focus this debut (or re-debut) was that its chapters should, however loosely, be tied to a particular theme. What grew from this general notion was an edition addressing the "re-generation" of the roots community. To a fair extent, the cover story of our March-April 2008 issue — a collective overview of the changes that were swirling around an impressive community of young string bands — served as a sort of blueprint for much of this inaugural bookazine.

Many of the bands discussed in that piece — including Crooked Still, the Duhks and the Infamous Stringdusters — were in the midst of lineup changes when the issue was printed, but had not yet sprung forth with the music which sprouted from those transitions. Over the summer months, each of them released new albums, and so the bookazine offered an opportunity to revisit those acts in-depth.

Another prime-subject of the string-band piece, Uncle Earl banjoist Abigail Washburn, teamed with Béla Fleck, Casey Driessen and Ben Sollee to release the first full-length disc under the name the Sparrow Quartet in May; in August, they traveled to Beijing to perform their ambitious musical melding of American and Chinese cultures at the Summer Olympics. We saw fit to make them the subject of our first cover, perhaps especially appropriate in that longtime banjo master Fleck is in some ways bridging the gap from one string generation to the next.

The rest of the content more or less followed suit, with one notable exception: Yes, *that* Hanson. Our longtime senior editor David Cantwell had been badgering us to write at length about the formerly chart-topping teen-pop trio for some time now (he'd reviewed their 2007 disc *The Walk* in our bimonthly pages),

and it occurred to us that they brought something unique to this youth-focused issue. While all three brothers are still in their 20s, they're also well-worn veterans of both the art and commerce of making music. They offered a perspective no other act in these pages could; and, besides, as Cantwell so deftly argues in 5,000-odd words here, their brand of bubble-gum power-pop is directly connected to the early roots of rock 'n' roll, as are the more traditionalist genres toward which we've generally gravitated in these pages.

Ah yes — *these pages*. They're still here, aren't they? It's good to have them back, and, more to the point, it's good to have *you* back as well. Stick around and we'll figure out exactly what we can do with a bookazine. Whatever that is.

— GRANT ALDEN
PETER BLACKSTOCK

The sun is hot, the earth is round, and musicians can't make a living playing music. There are truths to life. Which becomes easier to endure once people agree to accept them. Except Samantha Crain didn't buy into it. Crain was a sophomore at Oklahoma Baptist University, a Christian liberal arts school (enrollment 1,607) in Shawnee, Oklahoma — a tiny town of feed mills and flat vistas 35 miles from Oklahoma City — when she decided to drop out of school and "just do music for a living." This was despite the fact that she'd never toured, and had guitar skills that could be best described as negligible (she'd started playing only a year earlier).

"I don't know why," she said of the decision. "It seemed to come out of nowhere."

Her plans caused friction at home and confusion among her classmates, but two years later, Crain is still on the road. Now she's accompanied by a full band playing songs from *The Confiscation* (Ramseur Records), a debut EP of pretty folk pop traced by dark and damaged edges.

Despite Crain's insistence that she made a "a musical novella" and not an EP, and song titles which sound like they dropped off a Fall Out Boy album and were reworked by English grad students ("In Smithereens, The Search For Affinity"), the childish wonderment of Crain's world is best channeled through her voice. Like Joanna Newsom and, to an extent, Thom Yorke, Crain turns ordinary words into extraordinary sounds through an appealing vocabulary of ticks, slurs and accents. She says her singing developed organically, a result of not knowing what she was up to in the first place and trying to sound comfortable singing words.

"I always hated how my voice sounded when I talked," she said. "Everyone in my family, they either have this elegant accent that comes from their Native American [heritage] or they have these southern drawls. Everyone...has a real character to their accent; I just fell in-between."

Samantha Crain

Sings about the places where the dark and light of Oklahoma play

by Mark Guarino
photograph by Julie Roberts

Crain, 21, grew up in Shawnee to parents of Native American heritage. Her father owns a fitness gym in town and her mom is a third-grade teacher. Her education took place just outside town, in a school district surrounded by cornfields. Because Shawnee is built on reservation land, four different Indian casinos square off each side of town. "There's not a whole lot of stuff going on," she said. "It's just a town built around a feed mill."

She was writing short fiction in high school but felt uncomfortable reading what she produced out loud. So when her father gave her a guitar before she entered the college across town, she tried figuring out ways to transcribe them to music. "Whenever I picked up the guitar and sang along with it, I could make the words sound however I wanted," she recalled. "That made me feel more comfortable sharing any writing I had done."

The guitar became the outlet she needed. Shawnee's slow pace of life forced her imagina-

"She's a tiny, tiny young woman with a booming, loud,

tion to grow. As a child, she developed a knack for making up stories based on things she saw or heard around town; she would elaborate off the cuff, developing a style of writing that was grounded in earthly drama but could take flight to anywhere she desired.

By the time she made it to the Baptist university, her interest in music grew to a point that she had to temporarily exit her sophomore year to move to Martha's Vineyard for a semester long songwriter's camp. The experience widened the lens to what she needed: a community.

She also met Joey Lemon of the Chicago band Berry, who would later become a collaborator, producer and musical instigator. "Because we play completely different music, it works well in influencing each other," Crain says. "Joey has written a lot of folkier stuff and I have written weirder stuff since we met. It helps expanding our minds a little bit."

Lemon, 27, remembered that, while he was not knocked out as much by her early songs, Crain stood out for her sound. "She's a tiny, tiny young woman with a booming, loud, beautiful voice," he said.

Returning home but having decided to drop out of school, Crain started traveling to Oklahoma City to play more shows and build relationships with bands there. At home, things were not as bright. "Nobody wanted to talk about it; nobody really understood what I was doing for a good year and a half," she said. "People argued about it all the time."

She formed a duo with singer Beth Bombara, who also attended the program at the Vine-

Samantha Crain (center) cavorting with the Midnight Shivers (l. to r.) Andrew Tanz, Jacob Edwards, and Nate Henricks.

beautiful voice." — *Joey Lemon*

yard. The pair opened a month of shows for Lemon and then toured another month opening for his band. They played a sloppy mix of blues and garage noise, trading slide guitar, a marching-band drum kit, and the occasional pot and pan in a performance style that had as much to do with how it looked as much as how it sounded. "She obviously had a very unique thing going," Lemon says.

When later asked to produce *The Confiscation*, Lemon remembered those early performances and worked to transform the "shitty two-piece band I had been touring with for two months" into a richer setting that would benefit from the facilities of a four-piece lineup.

In the meantime, Crain learned how to book shows and approach labels, resulting in a lifestyle that leads her away from Oklahoma for nine months a year. Her EP eventually reached the ears of Dolph Ramseur, owner of the North Carolina indie label that bears his last name; he signed Crain and agreed to act as her manager. She has also fallen in with a four-piece band, the Midnight Shivers, that plays tougher versions of the tracks on *The Confiscation* but does not alleviate the weight of the songs' sorrowful heart.

"I'm a pretty outgoing happy person, but I think there's always this lingering sense of melancholy which I feel comes from most people who live in small towns," Crain suggests. "There's this lingering fog of sadness hanging over everyone. I'm not saying everyone is depressed and sad; it's just the feel of the area I grew up in — it's flat and barren. And everyone has this weird thing of, 'I wish I could get out of here but I don't really want to get out of here.' That's where the dark and the light meet."

Mark Guarino lives and writes in Chicago, Illinois.

PLANTS
AND BIRDS
BOWERBIRDS
AND ROCKS
AND THINGS
by DAVID MENCONI
photographs by
DEREK L. ANDERSON

An old-fashioned writing-class exercise asks you to analyze a piece of prose by cataloguing its nouns. So here's a sampling of what you pick up from the lyrics to the twelve songs on *Hymns For A Dark Horse* (Dead Oceans Records), the debut album from North Carolina trio Bowerbirds: moon, forest, wind, sparrow, soil, brook, warbler, beetle, thunder, fawn, pines, desert, mountains, dirt, frogs, snail. That's admittedly simplistic, but it still creates a very accurate picture of Bowerbirds as a band that's decidedly of and for this planet. Small wonder that one of the most-discussed lines on the album has been, "It takes a lot of nerve to destroy this wondrous earth" (from the song "In Our Talons").

"That line really bothers people," says singer/accordionist Beth Tacular over a fruit plate at a Raleigh coffeehouse. "Either they hate it, or they love it. Some people think it's hippie-dippie, the sort of thing most art is afraid to talk about. But remember, these songs were written three or four years ago — before IBM and everyone else 'went green.' Some people might think we're trying to jump on a bandwagon, but we're not. It's time to think about simplicity. We really are making it potentially impossible for humans to live on this planet anymore."

Of course, Bowerbirds' thanks-but-hold-the-electricity stance would be less likely to be heard if it were not couched in such beguiling music. The trio — Tacular, singer/guitarist Phil Moore and multi-instrumentalist Mark Paulson — crafts cinematic, quietly evocative soundscapes out of acoustic guitar, accordion, fiddle, loping drums, and the occasional autoharp. Deceptively simple, it's also deeply emotional, conjuring up images of secrets gleaned from the forest primeval.

Moore writes most of the lyrics, sounding a note of quiet desperation with stakes much

Flocking together (l. to r.): Mark Paulson, Beth Tacular, and Phil Moore.

higher than a mere relationship — as in the fate of the entire human race, foretold in apocalyptic language typically employed by romantic poets. Most Bowerbirds songs find the trio dramatically harmonizing on lines such as, "Ocean swells and roars with wild invention."

Tacular, who is Moore's romantic partner as well as his bandmate, says Moore does write some songs that begin as simple love ballads. But they never seem to end up that way. "You'll start writing songs like that, but then you'll change them," she says to Moore, who's sitting across the table. He seems to blush just a bit.

"It's not that I think songs like that are cheesy," he protests. "They're just not powerful to me. A simple I-love-you, moon-June song, that just doesn't do much for me. The world and what we're doing to it is kind of always on my mind, so it's what I write about. Beth is always reading some book that's blowing our minds — 'Wow, it could really be like that in another 20 years?!' — so it's disheartening."

Moore comes by his Earth-first tendencies honestly enough. Entering college at the University of Iowa, he knew he wanted to work outside. So he majored in biology, although it didn't take long for him to figure out that wasn't the career path for him (in part because it didn't accommodate his dual ambition in music very well). "I took some nonfiction writing classes during college, and I got better grades in those than in biology," he says. "By the end, I was skipping the biology, chemistry and physics homework to write. What I realized was that my original idea was just not going to work out, even though I tried to stick through this thing I'd chosen out of stubbornness. But I just wouldn't have the real-job opportunities I wanted."

Eventually, Moore wound up working as a bird-watcher in deepest South Carolina, living with Tacular in a schoolhouse in a forest. The isolated setting brought out a musical side of Moore that was quite different from his previous rock band, Ticonderoga. He began writing songs that called for a quieter, more measured approach.

At the time, Tacular was a painter rather than a musician. She taught herself to play accordion, and they formed Bowerbirds with Moore's Ticonderoga bandmate Paulson. *Hymns For A Dark Horse* (originally released in 2007 on Burly Time Records before being picked up by the Dead Oceans label this past June) quickly established the group as underground-folk darlings, especially after Mountain Goats main man John Darnielle raved about Bowerbirds as "beyond stunning…the complete package" on his blog (lastplanetojakarta.com). That put Bowerbirds on the road, although they've discovered just how tough it can be for a quiet band to tour.

"We played right down the street from Bob Mould in Minneapolis," says Tacular, laughing

technology in general..."   — *Phil Moore*

at the memory. "Between every song, you could hear him blaring away. Places like the church we played at South By Southwest [in Austin] are the best, spaces with natural reverb where people actually listen. Usually we're playing in a place that's basically a bar with people blabbing, air-conditioning blasting. There was this one place with a giant six-foot fan right behind us. They couldn't get my accordion mike to work, so they said, 'Just play loud so the vocal mike will pick it up.' I was pushing on it so hard, I gave my arms cramps."

Still, those bad gigs are getting fewer and farther between. The band's second full-length album is due in 2009, and Tacular describes it as upbeat and even "rowdy" (by Bowerbirds' standards). Thematically, however, it will be very much of a piece with *Hymns For A Dark Horse*.

"We were having this big discussion over lyrics the other night," Moore says. "Mark and Beth were asking me, 'What are you trying to do?' And they pointed out some changes in the lyrics, which I didn't even realize until we had this talk. Mark thinks the new songs aren't quite so didactic, and I'm trying to stray from that a little bit.

"But sometimes, yeah, I do feel forced to do a little finger-wagging. We seem to be relying on technology, whether it's solar or wind power, to save us and solve our problems. But can we really live like that? I think we probably need to rethink technology in general, to rethink...well, everything."

David Menconi was a longtime contributing editor for No Depression *magazine and is the music critic for the daily* Raleigh News & Observer.

Sarah Jarosz

Making friends in high lonesome places

by David Baxter

photographs by Scott Simontacchi

As an artist, it's always helpful to have a kindly advocate among your peers. Better still to have several. Speaking of her mentors, Sarah Jarosz rattles off half a dozen impressive names — Tim O'Brien, Darrell Scott, Mike Marshall, Chris Thile, Abigail Washburn, Aoife O'Donovan — before catching her breath. "Honestly, I could keep going on and on forever with names of people who've been inspiring me," she laughs. "I just feel really lucky."

The sense of admiration is mutual. Washburn has noted that Jarosz (pronounced juh-ROSE) is "full of virtuosity, passion, integrity, deep beauty, and soul." Scott is more direct: "She's just brilliant," he says.

The 17-year-old phenom from Austin, Texas, began singing at age 2, taking piano lessons at 6, and studying mandolin at 10. She added clawhammer banjo and guitar in her early teens. An only child, Jarosz is quick to acknowledge her parents' support. "They aren't stage parents — they've never pushed me to do music," she says. "They've always just encouraged me and done whatever it takes to get me to festivals and things like that." Her festival schedule for 2008 has been particularly rigorous, with appearances at SXSW, Bonnaroo, Telluride, RockyGrass, and Grey Fox, as well as various workshops, including David Grisman and Mike Marshall's Mandolin Symposium in Santa Cruz, California, and Dirk Powell's Fiddle Tunes in Port Townsend, Washington.

And Jarosz has been building relationships, even as she hones her musical talents. "This whole world of musicians," she says, "I've come to realize that it's kind of a small world." So along the way she has picked with the Greencards at Nashville's Station Inn, joined an impromptu hotel lobby jam with John Paul Jones and Uncle Earl, and shared the stage with Crooked Still at the Bowery Ballroom in New York City.

In the midst of this whirlwind schedule, she has also found time to begin recording her debut album — presently slated for a spring 2009 release on Sugar Hill Records — with Grammy-winning producer Gary Paczosa (John Prine, Chris Thile, the Duhks). Jarosz will play mandolin, banjo and guitar, and will be supported by many of the artists who inspired her. She anticipates doing two or three cover tunes, with the balance being original material.

"Everyone at Sugar Hill has been so encouraging and so supportive of my music and what I'm trying to accomplish as an artist," she says. "At this point in my life, it just feels like a really good fit for me. The label is really open-minded, as far as the music goes. And I feel like they're willing to be with me if I want to venture out and be as original as I can."

To be sure, Jarosz is not timid about venturing out. There are YouTube clips of her tack-

the better." — *Sarah Jarosz*

ling everything from the Beatles ("Drive My Car") to Tom Waits ("Come On Up To The House") to Gnarls Barkley ("Crazy"). Her interpretation of each tune is soulful and blues-drenched; none of it comes off as schtick.

"I've never been closed-minded to any type of music," Jarosz acknowledges. "I've always listened to as much music as I possibly can in any style. I just find that the more music I listen to, the more inspired I am and the more different types of influences I have running through me. So I listen to as many things as I can get my hands on."

Naturally, those stylistic influences eventually work their way into her repertoire. "If I'm going to do a cover, I like to be creative and find things that, maybe, people wouldn't necessarily think an acoustic musician would play," she says. "I've had really good feedback from doing those covers. It's always fun to do those songs, too."

One of the most captivating aspects of Jarosz's performance — more so, even, than her dazzling instrumental skills — is her voice. Perhaps the most apt description is this *non*-example: She does not sound like Alison Krauss. (In fact, she cites O'Brien and Scott as two of her primary vocal influences.) Full-throated, earthy and resonant, her sound is simply more mature, both sonically and emotionally, than one might expect from a 17-year-old.

Primarily because of her age and her instrument of choice, comparisons with Sierra Hull (a 17-year-old mandolinist whose debut album came out this year on Rounder) likely will be inevitable. On the other hand, Jarosz seems generally to be less traditional than Hull, who has an amazing command of bluegrass and newgrass music. Despite their similarities, the two artists largely operate in different musical spheres.

Consider the influences listed on Jarosz's MySpace page. Doc Watson and John Hartford are there, along with Nickel Creek and Old Crow Medicine Show. But so are Ella Fitzgerald and Nat King Cole. And the Decemberists. And Death Cab For Cutie. Conspicuously absent, however, are any references to Bill Monroe, Flatt & Scruggs, and the Stanley Brothers. Jarosz is quick to point out that she has spent a great deal of time listening to traditional bluegrass music — and she wonders aloud if she should revise her MySpace page. Still, her point of reference for old-time banjo technique wasn't the music of Dock Boggs or Roscoe Holcomb or Kyle Creed. It was Abigail Washburn's 2005 solo album *Song Of The Traveling Daughter*.

In the end, Jarosz is, wisely, more interested in expressing herself as an artist than in operating within the arbitrary confines of any genre. "I don't really know how to classify my music," she says. "I just write what I feel, and that's my original music that I create. Whatever I write is just me, and in creating this CD I'm just trying to represent myself and my music in the best way possible."

It is the very act of creation that drives Sarah Jarosz. And it is there that she finds her strongest connection to true artistry. "My favorite songwriters are really poets," she says. "The less they say, the better. There's no better feeling than writing a song. The feeling I get when I finish a song is just pure bliss. I live for that."

David Baxter teaches school, spins bluegrass on the radio, and writes in Bowling Green, Kentucky.

Top Secret

*Sierra Hull's debut album has marked her as
a rising star in bluegrass, complete with a role in a
Hollywood movie and a world tour. And then there's her senior prom,
back home in Byrdstown, Tennessee.*

by Silas House   photograph by Jim McGuire

Byrdstown is a community of about 900 people in the low, lush mountains of Middle Tennessee. There is one fast food restaurant, a Dairy Queen, and not a single stoplight. The Dollar General store and the Bobcat Den Cafe are usually pretty busy, but this summer day, it seems the whole town has been paralyzed by the heat. Beneath the broiling sun, cars idle slowly down the highway, where the blacktop steams beneath the white summer sky. Cicadas scream in the trees. Tiger lilies decorate the roadside in great clumps, but even these summer survivors are wilting a bit. It is the sort of day when only flies are foolish enough to venture out of the shade.

Days like this are gold mines for places like Byrdstown, though. The little city depends on tourists going down to nearby Dale Hollow Lake, renowned for its clear waters ("You can see all the way to the bottom in twenty foot of water," the cashier at the Save-A-Lot Grocery says, nodding for emphasis) and its great fishing: The world-record small-mouth bass was caught there in 1955, weighing in at 11 pounds, 15 ounces, and hasn't been topped since.

To take advantage of this tourist trade, the town elders here have wisely created several festivals that go on throughout the year. Chief among them are two events that are both named after Hulls. The first is the Cordell Hull Folklife Festival, named for the Byrdstown native who is largely responsible for the creation of the United Nations, for which he won the Nobel Peace Prize. The other is named for his distant cousin, 17-year-old Sierra Hull, who is most likely Byrdstown's most famous citizen of the moment. She doesn't have a Nobel Prize yet, but she does have an acclaimed album, *Secrets*, which was released in June by Rounder Records.

Secrets has been hailed as the emergence of a major talent by the likes of Alison Krauss, Adam Steffey and Sam Bush. Krauss calls Hull "remarkably talented." Bush says she is nothing less than "amazing." And Steffy, who has been named Best Instrumentalist five times by the International Bluegrass Music Association, names her as his favorite mandolin player. That's pretty high praise from musicians who are largely considered royalty in the arena of bluegrass music. Especially since Hull hasn't even graduated high school yet. The critics have sung her praises as well, anointing her as the kind of artist who could potentially put a bluegrass record on the mainstream charts. She's been compared to everyone from Krauss to Rhonda Vincent to Chris Thile.

Hull has a completely aw-shucks attitude about the accolades. "People can say things all they want, but I don't look at myself that way. I just appreciate everything," she says. "I just want to play music. And, at the same time, I want to be more than music. I want to be a good person." The amazing thing is that Hull doesn't sound like one of those prodigies who has been coached to talk in such a way. There's a genuine longing to be good in her voice which convinces the listener that she means it. And not only in her voice, but also in her drawl. Unlike so many teenagers across the modern south, she has refused to lose her accent. The misty coves and quiet pastures of Middle Tennessee are tucked away among her syllables and consonants. The place is a part of her, and she's already wise enough to recognize the positive aspects of that fact.

Her genuineness is also recognizable on her MySpace page, that all-important baring of the young person's soul. On there, she is down-home enough to post not only pictures of herself

music. I want to be a good person."   — *Sierra Hull*

balancing an orange juice bottle on her head while in class but also photos of her with her great-grandfather, and another one of her acting like she is sticking her finger up her father's nose. "My mando isn't the only thing I try to pick," she has written as the caption.

The revealing word there is "try." Only a musician with true modesty would say she "tries to pick" the mandolin after having done the things Hull has done. She's played the Grand Ole Opry, she was signed by the most prominent record label in bluegrass music, and she's getting ready to go international with a tour across Japan, having already been across the U.S. on the Great High Mountain Tour (which featured musicians from the *O Brother, Where Art Thou?* and *Cold Mountain* soundtracks). She's also a certified internet phenomenon, as evidenced by the more than 100,000 views that her rendition of "Roanoke" (with her former music teacher Carl Berggen) has garnered on YouTube, a website which contains nearly 40 videos featuring Hull.

Hull's parents would never let her get above her raising, though. "I have really good parents who keep my feet on the ground," she says. "They wouldn't allow any boastful behavior." She says they were never, ever stage parents. "Some parents can be overly encouraging, but instead they were always just encouraging and truthful. When I first started learning to play, my dad got excited, but they didn't really tell me I was special or anything."

Hull first picked up the mandolin at age 8, and she's barely laid it down since. She says she knew right away that playing music was what she wanted to do with her life. "I practiced all the time," she recalls. "I was just driven to play, to learn as much as I could." Her singing came naturally, too. She has never taken a singing lesson, yet her vocals are controlled and subtle, never overdone, always hitting just the right balance of emotion and precision.

Overwhelming musical talent doesn't really run in her family. She and her brother — two years her senior — used to sing in church, her parents always sang, and she says she can't remember a time when she wasn't surrounded by singing. Her great-uncle played mandolin and fiddle, and her father always wanted to play "but never had the chance," she says.

Sierra's mother, Brenda, a nurse, says she never would have dreamed that her marriage to Stacy Hull, who works in fiber optics, would produce a bluegrass prodigy, given his penchant for '80s rock music. Stacy worked away from home most of the week, but when he was home, he would often sit for hours and play rhythm guitar with Sierra while she practiced her mandolin. She started out by playing at small fairs and festivals. "My parents weren't big travelers at all, but they took me all over the place," she says.

One thing led to another. Before she knew it, she had been invited to play at an IBMA showcase, and by the time she was 11 she had the attention of Ken Irwin, co-founder of Rounder Records. "He sort of followed me around, watching me play, at the IBMAs," she says. "Even then he'd talk about making a record with me, but I was too young."

Irwin recalls one of those showcases clearly. "I stood by the stage one year at IBMA's World of Bluegrass where the younger musicians were taking turns getting up to play. Sierra was in line with about ten musicians, but she was totally involved and focused," he says. "She was quietly chopping her mandolin to the beat while the other musicians were playing, but then applauding and encouraging the others as they came off the stage. Onstage, she was totally comfortable in her own playing while supporting the other musicians she was playing with, smiling, nodding and quietly taking on a leadership role. She just *is* the complete package."

Without getting too caught up in all this sudden admiration, Hull kept plugging away at learning as much as she could about playing. Nowadays she still relishes those moments of simply practicing, climbing inside the music and losing herself. "When I'm playing onstage, I just concentrate on doing a good job," she says. "I'm in a whole different state of mind when I'm onstage, because I feel a big responsibility to do the best I can. But when I'm at home, just sitting on the porch, I can get completely relaxed, be at ease."

These days, being at home is a mixed blessing. Hull loves Byrdstown and would rather be with her family and friends than anywhere else. But the pull of the road is strong once you've had a taste of it. Sometimes, she says, she feels like she lives in two different worlds. "One day I'll be doing something completely amazing, singing somewhere that's so interesting and new, and then the next day, I'm in class, taking a test, and I'll realize, '*This* is reality,'" she says.

But although she understands her hometown life is separate from her music-career pursuits, she doesn't feel apart from it. "I recognize it as a different world," she says, "but I don't feel like a different person depending on where I am. I'm always the same."

Hull claims she's not treated any differently than anyone else in her hometown — despite having a whole music festival named for her — and she says her classmates have never given her a hard time about her life away from Byrdstown. "They've all been really encouraging and good to me. Maybe it's just where I live and all, but everybody at my school seems to like bluegrass and think it's cool to play that kind of music."

There's plenty to like on *Secrets*, which Hull co-produced with Ron Block, best-known as banjo player and guitarist for Alison Krauss & Union Station, but also an accomplished songwriter and burgeoning producer. Block says Hull had so many great ideas for the album that he felt compelled to list her as co-producer. "It was a matter of me facilitating what she already had inside of her," he explains. "She has a strong vision of her own."

Secrets is a star-studded affair, with appearances by such pickers as Dan Tyminski, Barry Bales, Jerry Douglas, Stuart Duncan, Tony Rice, Jim VanCleve, Rob Ickes, Chris Jones, Jason Moore, and 18-year-old banjo maestro Cory Walker, whom Sierra has known since she was about 9. But the show still belongs to Hull, whose vocals are highlighted throughout and whose playing is precise, energetic, and full of emotion. The album also includes three of Hull's own compositions, one written with her father. "I feel like *Secrets* totally represents the kind of music I love

and this album is about balance." — Sierra Hull

at this point," Hull says. "I'm a big Nickel Creek fan but I'm a big Doyle Lawson fan, too, and this album is about balance. I'm not much for labels; I believe in music."

Like most quintessential musicians, Hull views hard work as the key to making any kind of music good. "We worked as hard as we could on this album," she says. "I believe it's a record that I can always be proud of. Ron described it as 'setting a new standard,' and that's what you should always be doing, with each new album."

Rounder is supporting *Secrets* with a tour that will have Hull not only crossing the nation but also traveling across Japan. Her mother will accompany her, which she does as much as possible. Sierra says her parents are starting to let her do more things on her own, but usually only if Block is with her, as they consider him like family. For the trip to Japan, her mother has been preparing by reading up on the country as much as possible: "She wants to make sure we learn about the culture so we're not disrespectful," Sierra says.

Hull also will be on the big screen in the near future. She recently wrapped filming her scenes as Billy Graham's sister Catherine in the movie *Billy: The Early Years*, and she recorded "Just As I Am" and "I'll Fly Away" for the soundtrack, which is being produced by John Carter Cash. "It was just a few short lines," she says, though the Hollywood publication *Variety* lists her as one of the stars. Regardless, she'd rather be behind a mandolin than a camera any day. "I loved doing it, but when we wrapped for the day, I just wanted to play so bad, since I hadn't been able to all day long," she says. "So in the car on the way home I just got out my mandolin and played all the way home. That's what my heart is set on."

Her eyes, however, are set on the future. As she enters her senior year in high school, she looks forward to her prom, especially since she had to miss her junior prom so she could perform at Merlefest in North Carolina. She's also eager to record another album. "I learned so much on the first one that I'm ready to make another one," she says, though she estimates she won't find time to even consider recording for at least another year. After graduation, she hopes to move closer to Nashville (Byrdstown is a couple hours away), and to be on the road more often.

And while the constant comparisons to Krauss and Thile don't faze her — "I *have* been influenced by both of them," she says — she is also sure that eventually people will recognize her more for her own sound. "As much as I love them both, I want to be myself," Hull says. "I believe as I go on, those people who compare us will finally recognize my music as mine, as just being Sierra music. I'm still finding what I want to sound like."

In the meantime, she's perfectly happy here in Byrdstown, where the call of the road may be louder, but certainly isn't as satisfying as the sound of the cicadas clicking in the trees near the lake, or the ring of her mandolin's strings from her own front porch.

Longtime ND *contributing editor Silas House lives across the border in Kentucky but has been camping on Dale Hollow Lake every year since he was nine months old.*

The three siblings of the Homemade Jamz Blues Band have dug into the deep groove of Mississippi's rich tradition...with a little help from their parents.

the FAMILY THAT PLAYS TOGETHER, STAYS TOGETHER

by EDD HURT

photographs by Ebet Roberts

Hip, home-schooled kids who sing and play the blues, the three siblings who make up the Homemade Jamz Blues Band are, above all, amazingly polite. I pose a question, and it's "yes, sir" immediately, with a sense of proportion that is refreshing after the laconic, slipshod soundbites you often get from older, more jaded musicians. The Homemade Jamz members give answers that are well-thought-out, positive and casual.

It's morning in Tupelo, Mississippi, where Kyle, Ryan and Taya Perry make their home with their parents, Renaud and Tricia. When I ask 16-year-old Ryan how he's doing, he declares, "I'm doing really good, eatin' a good breakfast." The group has just come off the road, having done dates in Maine and New Jersey and a National Public Radio interview in Washington, D.C., before heading back to northeast Mississippi, which connects with Memphis via old U.S. Highway 78, heading west into the top of the big, rich, leaf-shaped Mississippi Delta region.

The trio's debut, *Pay Me No Mind*, came out in June on the Canadian label NorthernBlues, and it proves these youngsters know their stuff, even if they live in a pleasant, smallish Mississippi town known chiefly for furniture-making and being the birthplace of Elvis Presley. Ryan, the oldest of the three, is the leader; he plays guitar and sings, while bassist Kyle, 14, backs him up along with Taya, 10, who has been playing drums "almost three years," as she replies. These children of the blues have won big-time competitions, passed every audition, and made it look like a breeze, even though they admit to the nervousness that adult attention and success has a way of dispelling.

Still, as Tricia explains, Tupelo isn't a blues town. "Tupelo is unfriendly to musicians, is, I guess, a good way of putting it," she says. "I mean, it's a growing community, but there are still a lot of things they're not hip to. Versus, if we would drive two hours to Clarksdale or to Memphis — that's a musician's world, you know what I'm saying?" They've played in Memphis, with shows at Isaac Hayes' now-closed Peabody Place restaurant, on Beale Street, and at the annual Folk Alliance gathering. They got a gig at a prime Clarksdale club by winning over its owner with an audition at his folk-art shop. They've even played the Netherlands' Kwadendamme Blues Festival, a rite of passage for ambitious American blues acts seeking to expand their circuit.

But Tupelo is where it all began. "When we first started, we played at, of all things, a Mexican restaurant," Ryan remembers. "Played at a local bar there, right across the street, and decided not to do that anymore. There's no blues clubs and there's really no 'club' clubs. We have an Elvis festival, but they haven't called us to do that."

Ryan first became interested in playing guitar in Germany, where the family lived for a couple of years. (Renaud served in the U.S. Army and drove a truck for a Tupelo Lowe's store before he and Tricia, who worked at Northeast Mississippi Medical Center, quit their jobs to manage the band full-time.) "Me and my brother were born in Hawaii, and my sister was born in Maryland," Ryan says. "My dad was born here, though." Tricia grew up on American Samoa and on the west coast, where, she says, she didn't hear much blues music.

"My dad always listened to the blues when he came home," Ryan says. "Actually, that's when I first recognized it, in Germany. My dad would come home and change into his civilian clothes, and listen to the blues, and I was listening to them right along with him. In fact, I have all the CDs that he had — they're in my room now. He had John Lee Hooker, Muddy Waters,

Albert King, and he was big into Stevie Ray Vaughan, B.B. King and Little Milton, and T-Bone Walker and Johnny Guitar Watson."

It was a decent primer in blues guitar. Kyle cites a similar list: "I like Willie Dixon, B.B. King, [Alabama singer and guitarist] Willie King, Albert King and Muddy Waters." When you think about it, it's remarkable that an American teenager in the current era would have any conception of blues beyond, say, the ubiquitous B.B. King or the canonized Vaughan.

It also says something about the evolution of the form that this Tupelo family has cast its lot with such an old, raffish branch of this country's music. And while *Pay Me No Mind* has its share of voodoo women, jealous men, and lovers who climb every mountain and cross every sea (as on "Right Thang Wrong Woman"), the Perrys aren't making any pacts with the bluesy devils of yore.

"We're trying to put out something you can buy in the record store and listen to with your kids in the car," Ryan says. The lyrics on the album's ten originals, written by Renaud from what often sounds like a slightly incongruous adult perspective, work safely within the bounds of blues imagery. "Voodoo Woman" is about a female you'd think twice about introducing to your mother and father: "My mama told me, people/You better let that little girl alone."

And anyway, the magic of *Pay Me No Mind* lies in its pure striving, so it probably doesn't matter that you can't easily understand the words to "Voodoo Woman." (One couplet sounds something like, "She carried me onto the doll/I said, 'Leave if you get a change,'" which obviously isn't correct). If the classical purity of a Chess or Stax recording eludes the young trio, their energy and devotion to the form shine through here, just as it presumably did for Roger Stolle, the owner of Clarksdale's Ground Zero Blues Club, when the trio auditioned for him a couple years ago at Cat Head, the local blues and folk art store Stolle and his wife moved from St. Louis to open.

Homemade, indeed (l. to r.): Ryan, Taya, and Kyle Perry.

"It was really nervous," Ryan says of the audition. "We set up the equipment in front of the store, and we thought nobody was going to listen to us. But we actually had a good crowd and we did a good job, and the owner, Mr. Roger Stolle, came up and asked us later if we wanted to play at Ground Zero, and that's how it all started." (Stolle wound up writing the liner notes for *Pay Me No Mind*.)

The group won 2006's Mississippi Delta Blues Challenge, held in Indianola. At the following year's International Blues Challenge in Memphis, they took second place in the band category. In a list of finalists that included such bands as Iowa's Juke Joint Sinners, the group stood out for their verve, determination and sheer youthfulness.

Despite the thrill fans must feel when they behold an under-age trio pulling off a convincing take on post-'60s blues styles, there are times on *Pay Me No Mind* when the group's lack of experience tells on them, if slightly. Ryan's vocals are gritty and never excessive, but he often sounds as if he's simply being "bluesy" without much of a guiding principle. "Who Your Real Friends Are" finds him shouting "Hey!" and "Whoa!" a few too many times. For that matter, whether or not Ryan, at 16, possesses the kind of life experience that justifies his delivery of the song's world-weary lyrics is an interesting question.

Homemade Jamz, proving they're tuff enuff for the blues.

Produced by Miles Wilkinson in Tupelo and Nashville, *Pay Me No Mind* sounds clear and uncluttered. "The CD turned out really great," Ryan says. "The sound was good and we couldn't complain about anything." He says the group has also recorded a cover of Junior Wells' "Come On In This House" at a Clarksdale studio with veteran guitarist Elvin Bishop. The track will be included on Bishop's *The Blues Rolls On*, set for fall release; the collection also features George Thorogood, James Cotton and B.B. King.

Pay Me No Mind documents a band still learning its craft. Sometimes playing a guitar made by his father from a car muffler — that's where the "homemade" tag starts to make even more sense for this band — Ryan does a good simulation of the styles of Vaughan, Hendrix and Albert King. "Time For Change" sports a respectable guitar solo, while Ryan displays an ear for the major-sixth chords T-Bone Walker and other jazz-influenced blues players used. It's Ryan's show, and one gets the sense his siblings follow his lead.

This creates some problems, especially with Taya's drumming. After all, she's only 10, and on the evidence of *Pay Me No Mind*, she hasn't quite learned to play a straight shuffle. Rather, she kicks around the beat like a punk-rock drummer. She attempts cymbal work on "Who Your Real Friends Are," but it doesn't go anywhere, and her off-beats are distracting. She's slightly sluggish on "Time For Change." In general, the trio doesn't play in the kind of strict time you'll hear on, say, Albert King's Stax recordings with drummer Al Jackson Jr. In fact, "Penny Waiting On Change" features more turns within its five minutes than the disciplined Jackson probably

everything." — Taya Perry

permitted in his entire career. The adherence to, and respect for, straight time is what has always separated good blues from mediocre; you can hear it in the Albert King recordings and on performances featuring Fred Below, the masterful drummer who played on countless Chess Records sides by the likes of Sonny Boy Williamson.

The Homemade Jamz Blues Band have their own, somewhat coltish energy, and it's best sampled on the album's title track, where Taya's straightforward beats mix with Renaud's harmonica and some nicely executed stop-time passages for a completely satisfying performance. They're playing blues as a form that has been codified, and while the execution isn't always elegant, their playing isn't about pushing boundaries. As Ryan puts it, "I believe [blues] is the best form you can play an instrument to, and that style of playing I grew into when I started and came natural to me, because I was listening to it most of my childhood."

For Kyle, it's somewhat simpler: "My brother and me and my sister make the music and my dad writes the lyrics," he says. Like Taya, he sees nothing particularly exotic or retro in their choice of genre, so he doesn't worry about what his friends might think of their embrace of this supposedly archaic musical style. "I don't think they really care," he offers. "They ask, 'Where you playin' at next?' and everything, but it's cool with them."

Taya says she listens to "a little bit of Hannah Montana, and I wouldn't exactly say rap," which makes her a reassuringly typical pre-teen pop fan. As for her friends, she says, "They actually kinda want to be me, because I get to travel all over the world and get to make new friends every single time. They say, 'Hey, where'd you go? Can I come with you?' They like me, and actually support me."

Far from being the lonely torchbearers of tradition, as were the blues fanatics of 40 years ago, the Perrys see their mission — if they think in those terms — as simply being good entertainers. Ryan sounds proud when he tells me how he overcame his stage fright ("I even crack a couple of jokes onstage," he says), and Tricia seems concerned with balancing the demands of the road with making sure her kids grow up right. "I still manage them as children and make sure they do what they're supposed to do and get what they need for it," she says.

For all that, the eternal questions remain, and maybe the group will answer some of them along the way. When I ask Taya where she thinks the blues came from, she gives me as sensible an answer as you're likely to hear anywhere in the Magnolia State, not to mention the Netherlands. "The blues comes from everything," she says. "But I think the blues came from Clarksdale, 'cause, I mean, the club we always go to, there's a lot of big famous people that go there and play."

ND contributing editor Edd Hurt first heard blues on childhood hunting and fishing trips in West Tennessee. A writer and pianist whose left-hand technique could bear improving, he currently makes his home in Nashville, which is more of a blues town than it likes to admit.

Each life converges to some centre

A life in music found Basia Bulat, and she answered the call

by Peter Blackstock
photograph by Anthony Seck

The first thing that impresses about Basia Bulat's music is its...maturity. Which is not to suggest she's overly serious; indeed, a YouTube viewing of her video for "In The Night," a song on her debut album *Oh, My Darling*, features Bulat dancing around with friends who are dressed in animal and skeleton costumes. Clearly, this Canadian singer-songwriter still revels in the opportunity to have plain and unabashed fun.

But few 24-year-old musicians come across as unforced and self-assured as Bulat does on *Oh, My Darling*. Its songs sound like they could have been around for decades — not in a revivalist or throwback sense, but something more fundamental. They simply feel second-nature, like you must've known them all your life. That's rare territory for an artist to reach, especially their first time on record.

Take, for example, "I Was A Daughter," the disc's second track. The anchoring guitar strum that opens the song gradually is augmented by other elements — minimalist piano accents, an infectiously rhythmic round of handclaps, then Bulat's richly emotional voice, and finally strings that fully flesh out the song's melody. By the time the building tension breaks halfway through, with everything but Bulat's voice and delicate plucks of strings and plinks of piano dropping away, the song has already settled in deep. The quiet pause proves dramatically dynamic, setting things up for one last rush to its conclusion: "We gave away our hearts before we knew what they were," Bulat sings, then repeats those last three words, three times, her voice reaching ever higher with each pass, the strings and handclaps returning, swirling and soaring to a shimmering crescendo around her. It's breathtaking, it's brilliant, and it's all over in less than three minutes. And I swear this song was somehow in my soul long before I heard it.

That sensation is far from an isolated incident of transcendence on *Oh, My Darling*. "Snakes And Ladders" and "In The Night" weave similar spells, if more stridently, with full drums replacing handclaps and indelible piano runs reinforcing the melody. On the quieter side, "Little One" recalls the finest of classic English folk-rock, from the beckoning violin solo that opens the track to Bulat's brooding and beguiling minor-key vocal turn in the chorus. Perhaps the album's most perfectly captured moment — indelible enough that fan-performed versions of the song have started to pop up on YouTube — is the opening track, "Before I Knew," which says all it needs to say in barely over a minute. Ukulele strums and clapping rhythms accompany Bulat as she sings: "The first time I felt my heart/Was the first time I sang out loud, all through the night/But before I knew, I was lost." A chorus of voices harmonizes with her on the song's title words, lifting her up from the lyrics of despair. It's so spare, it's almost primal, and that's a big part of Bulat's charm.

"I definitely do appreciate finding open spaces in the small space, and being able to open up a lot more with a lot less," Bulat says, when asked about the relative brevity of her songwriting on *Oh My Darling*; all but two cuts are under four minutes, and a couple clock in at less than a minute and a half. "That's why I really love Emily Dickinson so much, because she can do in four lines what some people can't do in a novel."

That Bulat — whose first and last names are pronounced BOSH-uh boo-LOT — would reference Dickinson is not too surprising, given that she was studying English literature at the

four lines what some people can't do in a novel." — *Basia Bulat*

University of Western Ontario in London, Ontario, when *Oh, My Darling* redirected her future plans. (She'd earned her undergraduate degree and was working on a Master's; she says she plans to finish eventually, joking that her professors "are willing to take me back as a student whenever my next record flops!") She made the album in Montreal in 2006 while spending time there learning French as part of her academic studies; former Arcade Fire drummer Howard Bilerman produced it, and helped find the album a home with Rough Trade Records. The U.K.-based label released it overseas in spring 2007; a Canadian release (on Hardwood Records) followed that fall before Rough Trade issued it in the U.S. in early 2008.

Bulat was raised in Toronto (where she recently returned to live), and was well-grounded in music from an early age — her mother was a classical piano teacher — although she didn't quite foresee touring the continent and beyond as a singer-songwriter. "I always knew that music was always going to be very important in my life," she says. "That was something that was perhaps non-negotiable. Music and books — those are the two things that I really love the most. So I just always found some way to either play with other people, or sing, or do the radio show on campus and just be around people who appreciate music."

Growing up, Bulat learned to play piano — "when I was really little, I wanted to be a concert pianist," she recalls — and in high school played upright bass as well as flute. That instrumental variety served her well when she started making her own music; not only has she continued to add to her own repertoire (in concert, she plays autoharp as well as acoustic guitar), but she tends to be broad-minded and innovative in terms of writing and arranging.

"I get excited by the fact that there might be something new and fun to play in the room," she says. "A lot of the instruments, they transfer over, like the guitar, the bass, and the ukulele; they're not the same, but they have similar principles that apply. And the flute and the saxophone, the fingerings are kind of the same. I don't think I'm necessarily amazing at anything, but I do feel like I can at least play a song or write a song on almost anything."

That open-ended instrumental mindset carries over to her live performances. Bulat's touring lineup frequently features such uncommon components as ukulele and viola in addition to more typical instruments such as piano and drums. Her sound is a far cry from standard two-guitars-bass-drums fare, and all the more intriguing for that. "Those are the instruments I like and wanted — not necessarily to be different from anybody," she explains. "A lot of the music that I listen to sometimes will be just a guitar and a banjo and a ukulele and voices or something. With folk music, it's not necessarily that unusual, but maybe it's strange that we don't have a bass. Sometimes we have a cello with us, and that kind of acts as the bass....Those are sounds that speak to me a little more; somehow it seems like that's what needs to be there."

In particular, it's hard to imagine many of the songs on *Oh, My Darling* without the string-section support that adds a great deal of grace and depth. "When I was making the record, it was really very much just trying to document what my friends and I were doing at the time with these songs," she says. "And we did have a string trio basically playing with me at all my shows in London" during her college days.

The string presence has continued to figure heavily in her approach to songwriting, Bulat says, judging from the material she's written to date for her next record. "With some songs, I know that there can't be a lot extra there — like it's just autoharp and voice, or guitar and voice, or piano and drums and voice," she notes. "But I'd say about 70 percent of the songs I write, I'm thinking about how I want the strings to sound — not even whether I want them or not, but just, OK, what are they actually going to play. It's just a given. It's not like a 'production' thing; it's like, no, this is what has to *be* there."

The time for arranging and recording that new material is likely coming soon, seeing as how it's now been two years since *Oh, My Darling* was made. "I think I have probably eighteen or nineteen [songs]," she says. "I have a lot. There's still a lot of work that needs to be done, and who knows, maybe I'll write another eighteen more before I even get into the studio."

There's also the possibility of putting her own stamp on other writers' songs. Hints of Bulat's talents as an interpreter have shown through on a recent 7-inch single featuring a cover of soul legend Sam Cooke's "Touch The Hem Of His Garment," as well as on an enchantingly ramshackle reading of the Strokes' "Someday" which has been posted to her MySpace site for several months. "That's from a practice that we did, from like 2005, that I've been meaning to take down," she says. "But everyone's like, 'You can't take it down!'"

Perhaps her finest cover to date, though, is an autoharp rendition of Daniel Johnston's

that is true to myself." — *Basia Bulat*

"True Love Will Find You In The End," which she has been playing frequently in her live shows for a good while. First covered by Johnston's fellow Austinites the Reivers way back in 1987 — shortly after it had appeared on Johnston's independent cassette release *Retired Boxer* — the song has gained considerable traction in recent years via versions by Wilco (as a B-side to a late-'90s single) and Beck (on the Johnston tribute album *Discovered Covered*).

As fate would have it, Bulat's voice — compared at times to Sandy Denny and Natalie Merchant, and creatively described by one writer as being like "demerara," a light-brown raw sugar often used in making rum — in fact is quite closely akin to that of Kathy McCarty, who in 1995 recorded an entire album of Daniel Johnston songs.

To Bulat, "True Love Will Find You" is a standard-in-the-making. "Some songs I just think need to be sung out a lot more," she suggests. "I was thinking about how so many people were covering each others' songs in the '60s and '70s — it was just sort of like, that's how the song earned its 'standard' stripes, was how many people played it. And I definitely think some songs *deserve* to be standards. I think everybody should know that Daniel Johnston song."

Bulat has her own personal tale as to how she became aware of Johnston's music. "I actually met him very briefly," she relates. "He was opening for Yo La Tengo. It was in Toronto, at this place called the Phoenix; I must have been like 18. And the Phoenix had this little room where there was a pay-phone and they'd sell pizza and stuff. At the time I was just calling my mom to get a ride home, and he [Daniel] was there. And I said something like, 'That was a good show.' I was a little bit intimidated, because it's an artist, and he's, you know, a big guy, and I was 18. And he said something like, 'Thanks, can I buy you a slice of pizza?' It was so strange, like this bizarre, surreal moment: Daniel Johnston offering to buy me a slice of pizza."

In the end, for Bulat, what she hears in Johnston's songs is what she's constantly striving to achieve with her own writing. "What I'm always trying to do is find something that is true to myself," she says. "Not necessarily a universal truth or anything like that. But I definitely feel like, when you're listening to him, you know who he is. It's not a facade. I think the reason why so many people admire him is because of that — because you can hear his heart."

ND co-editor Peter Blackstock bought a copy of Daniel Johnston's Retired Boxer *cassette from Waterloo Records in Austin, Texas, in 1986. It was recorded on bargain-basement-quality tape, and it still plays, two decades later.*

a CHIP off HIS OWN BLOCK

*In a town with no shortage of blues-guitar greats,
Austin's Gary Clark Jr. has risen to the fore
as a singular kind of player.*

by Michael Hoinski
photograph by Todd V. Wolfson

"...when you get an opportunity like that, you've got to at least try

"**S**omeone asked him the other day, 'What do you want for your birthday?'," the emcee says of boogie-woogie piano player Pinetop Perkins, who is celebrating his 95th birthday at Antone's, Austin's holy grail of blues clubs, on a sticky night in early July. Pinetop's response, as per the emcee: "A pair of red shoes." On cue, handlers help Pinetop ascend the stage, where he is lauded with claps and at least one "Pinetop, we love you!" He is wearing red shoes, all right. He is also wearing a red suit and a red fedora. Red from toe to head. It's as if he's giving his final shout-out to the devil, to whom he sold his soul back in the day in exchange for wicked skills, like many a fabled bluesman before him. Adding to that train of thought is the emcee's revelation that the suit was a gift from Ike Turner, a dancer with the devil if ever there was one.

Clifford Antone, the deceased club owner who arguably did as much for black-white race relations as Mark Twain, marvels from a giant picture on the wall as Pinetop receives citations. At some point after it is acknowledged just how cool it is for a blues cat such as Pinetop to play out his remaining days in Austin instead of, say, Chicago, the frail but beaming birthday boy whispers something into the emcee's ear.

"Pinetop's asked me three times," the emcee says to the crowd: "'Where's the band? Where's the band? Where's the band?'"

The hoopla is getting to Pinetop. Standing there in that red suit is giving him the itch. He's burning up. He wants to jam. He wants to lock and load onstage with "The Future," Gary Clark Jr., before the devil suddenly pulls the plug.

Clark is the featured player in Pinetop's makeshift, four-piece backing band this evening. Earlier this year, the 25-year-old Austin-born-and-bred guitar phenom made his acting debut as Sonny in John Sayles' *Honeydripper*. In the film, Clark portrays a savior in the guise of a blues rocker based on Guitar Slim, whose routine breaking of the fourth wall Gary conveys, and Bo Diddley, whose box-like electric guitar Gary draws raucous notes from. "The madness" is what Gary, in our interview a week prior to Pinetop's birthday, called the movie's premiere, which took place at the Paramount Theatre in Austin on a cold January night. Ever since, Gary's no longer been known as just one of Cliffy's kids, or as just the free happy-hour opener for the Jon Dee Graham-James McMurtry doubleheader that takes place every Wednesday at the Continental Club on South Congress Avenue, or as just the go-to guitar-slinger for old-school blues musicians needing a helping hand, like Pinetop. Indeed, the silver screen made him a double threat, and that put a shine on his blues.

Pinetop, all twinkle-eyed behind his spectacles, is sizing up Gary from his piano bench on the opener, "Down In Mississippi." Clark is roughly 6-foot-5, but too lanky and nonchalant to intimidate. His fingers are Twizzlers that contort across the neck of his Fender Strat like a Cirque du Soleil freakshow during a Chuck Berry-esque solo. He's wearing a white V-neck T-shirt and sports the slightest afro. Flanking him are guitarist Derek O'Brien, whom Clark studies in order to pick up the rhythm, and bassist Ronnie James; behind him is drummer Jay Moeller, who also plays with Clark in his own band. Pinetop is downstage to Gary's left, at a 45-degree angle that allows him the best seat in the house for Gary's razzle-dazzle playing on "They Call Me Pinetop Perkins" and "Big Fat Mama."

and step up, you know?"   — *Gary Clark Jr.*

Clark looks like a natural because he is, and he's played enough pickup games with pros like Pinetop to have the drill down pat. He knows how to watch, learn, and adapt on the fly. He's already felt the laser stare of the VIP onlookers upstairs. The picture on the wall of Muddy Waters, with whom Pinetop came of age, ain't no thang to him. You'd have to go back ten years ago, when Gary, 15, made his Antone's debut, to understand this supernatural facility.

"It was pretty crazy," Clark says in his shy and laconic way. He's sitting out front of Guero's Taco Bar, the epicenter of South Congress, on a sweltering day a week prior to Pinetop's party — and he's wearing a faded Antone's T-shirt. "I went in and Hubert Sumlin was playing with Mojo Buford, and James Cotton was playing...Tommy Shannon was on bass, Chris Layton was on drums, and Cliff was like, 'Hey, you wanna get up and play?' I go, 'All right.'"

"So when you're 15 are you fearless?" I ask.

"No. Hell no. I was pretty scared. My voice was shaking and palms were sweating and all that kind of stuff. But when you get an opportunity like that, you've got to at least try and step up, you know?"

Gary Clark Jr. saving the day in Honeydripper.

That opportunity was afforded him by Eve Monsees, his running buddy since third grade. She now fronts a '50s-style rock band called Eve & the Exiles and occasionally plays with former Go-Go's bassist and Austin native Kathy Valentine. A couple days after Pinetop's party, in an interview independent of my chat with Gary, she recounts how she met Clifford at a Jimmie Vaughan show at Antone's to which her dad had brought her, and how she and Gary subsequently ended up onstage with the aforementioned legends before they were old enough to drive.

"I met Clifford and said something about, 'Oh, yeah, I play guitar, and I like the blues,'" Eve says. "He gets *how* many people coming up to him and telling him that? But he says, 'So what do you listen to?' He's probably thinking I'm gonna say, you know, Jimi Hendrix or Eric Clapton. I said Magic Sam, who's kind of this obscure blues player, and he kind of paused and put his head in his hands and kind of shook his head. And I'm like, 'What did I do?' And he's like, 'Wow, that's great. We'll have to get you up and play.'"

Eve is buoyant and talkative and the total opposite of Gary. She's in a coffee shop next door to Antone's Record Shop, the utopia for black vinyl north of the University of Texas cam-

"He's as solid a player as anybody I've ever played with. He's got a stone-cold,

pus; she's worked at the store since high school. The coffee shop is playing her band's new CD, *Blow Your Mind*. She just got copies earlier in the day. She leaves tomorrow morning to go play a blues festival in Finland. She's super-stoked.

She and Gary grew up a block away from each other in Oak Hill on the southwest outskirts of Austin. She was the first to get a guitar, an acoustic when she turned 12. A year later she graduated to a Strat. Gary quickly followed suit with his own electric, and the two began figuring out and teaching each other as much as they could, all the while listening to the likes of Freddie King and Albert King and the Ramones.

"I knew a few things before he did," says Monsees. "I kind of showed him the little bit that I knew, and he started learning from a book. He was definitely very quick to learn. I mean, I thought I picked up on things pretty quickly but, that said, you know, he was that much quicker."

Back at Guero's, the same subject matter elicits this response from Clark: "Some people learn differently, and I'm just one of those people who doesn't really have the patience to, like, just read off the page, or whatever. I just listen to it and try and mimic it, you know?" He shrugs and averts his eyes. "I don't know how that works."

Leading up to that fateful night at Antone's, Gary and Eve honed their chops at open-band nights at Babe's, a now-defunct joint on Sixth Street in downtown Austin. There they found comfort in the blues idiom and learned how to play off of other musicians, thanks to the house bassist and drummer. They also developed their own musical vocabulary.

"Our folks would both come," Monsees recalls. "They would both videotape it. And, you know, I had just turned 15 and Gary's 14. It was a real thrill for us. We weren't very good, but..."

Nowadays, Clark is a regularly gigging soloist and power-trio frontman. He released three small-label albums to no fanfare, really, before getting on the *Honeydripper* soundtrack. At 18, he put out his trad-blues debut, *Worry No More*. Next up was *110*, a precocious amalgamation of blues, soul, and R&B. *Tribute* is an offering of live cuts. His next album, the one that'll come out on the heels of the movie, figures to be his first legit shot for expansion into the national market. Trouble is, he can't finish it.

"I've been nearing completion for awhile," Clark says. "But I'm doing most of the stuff at my house, so I'm always making changes. I need someone to come and unplug all my shit, and be like, 'That's it.'"

Clark doesn't get into many specifics about the new, as-yet-untitled album with no set release date. What he does offer is that it's pretty different from its predecessors.

lowdown groove." — Chris Layton

"There's not a whole lot of blues on it," he says. "It's kind of more…like, I grew up listening to the Motown stuff, like Marvin Gaye, and I'm kind of a product of the '80s, with all that weird stuff kind of influencing me. So I'm just kind of letting that stuff out."

Variations on two songs from the new album were available on Clark's MySpace page in mid-summer. "Don't Owe You A Thang" is an uptempo roadhouse rocker about a man keeping his freedom from a woman, and "Can't Sleep At Night" is a dance tune about a man who can't give up his freedom to a woman fast enough.

Clark plays all of the instruments — guitar, bass, drums, synthesizer, trumpet, samplers, etc. — on these and other prospective tracks. The songs are influenced by who he's been listening to lately: Curtis Mayfield, Prince, his parents' records. They're also influenced by the limitations of the blues. "I'm trying to write a lot," he says, "and it's kind of hard to say a whole, whole lot in a 1-4-5 blues-standard format, you know, so I'm breaking out of that."

Side projects such as Frogleg, a funk collective with grooves in the vein of the J.B.'s and Grant Green, are good forums for Clark to practice such deviation. Chris Layton, the drummer in Frogleg, has also played in the shadows of a host of other godly guitarists, including Buddy Guy, Charlie Sexton, and Stevie Ray Vaughan. He can separate the wheat from the chaff.

"I like the idea that, you know, Gary Clark seems to be the first Gary Clark and not the second somebody else," Layton says in a thick drawl over the phone from Lansing, Michigan, where he's on tour with Kenny Wayne Shepherd. Layton goes on and on about Clark's natural ability, having played with him in various configurations since that night at Antone's ten years ago. (Monsees is positive that it was a different drummer, but Clark and Layton outnumber her.) "He's as solid a player as anybody I've ever played with," Layton says. "He's got a stone-cold, lowdown groove. You know, it's a hard thing to describe; you know it when you play with somebody and you feel it from 'em. But he just has a great groove. He sings like a bird, and he just plays his ass off."

That's exactly what Clark is doing onstage at Antone's, and that's probably exactly what Pinetop is thinking about him as the first set comes to an end. "The Future" appears infinitely comfortable in his own skin. His body language is totally laid-back. He lets things come to him. In a celebration of the beginning of his promising career, the latter days of Pinetop's storied career, and the shape of the blues to come, the duo sing in unison over and over and over, "Got my mo-jo working," while Clifford Antone taps his toe up above.

Michael Hoinski is an Austin-based freelancer whose writing also appears in The New York Times, Village Voice, *and* RollingStone.com, *among others. For more info: www.MichaelHoinski.com.*

PORT

FOLIO

Though they endured modest pay and, in the early days, very bad reproduction, *No Depression* has been lucky enough to work regularly with several dozen of the finest music photographers in the world.

For this new bookazine thing (whatever it is), we asked our core contributors to participate in a group photo essay, celebrating young roots music makers. We didn't define young, nor roots, nor how old the photos should be.

We just asked what we always ask: For their best. And, as always, they gave it. Willingly.

Enjoy. As always, we are grateful.   —*grant alden*

AT LEFT: *Jon Bertrand and the Pine Leaf Boys (Drew Simon on drums, Blake Miller on bass), celebrating his 25th birthday at Tipitina's in New Orleans, Louisiana, January 14, 2007. Photograph by Erika Molleck Goldring.* **ABOVE:** *Neko Case, cruising around Tacoma, Washington, with two of her Boyfriends, ca. 2001. Photograph by Alice Wheeler.*

LEFT: *Marketa Irglova of Swell Season at Noe Valley Ministry, San Francisco, California, August 5, 2007. Photograph by Tom Erikson.* **ABOVE:** *Warren Hood of the Waybacks, on the main stage at Merlefest, April 26, 2007. Photograph by Jon Hancock.*

ABOVE: *These folks call themselves Trey Deuce (after a long-running domino league). Each member leads his or her own band (among them: Sad Apartment, Ole Mossy Face, Hands Down Eugene, and Duraluxe); everybody plays with everybody. They assembled in July, 2008 at Thomas Petillo's Nashville, Tennessee, studio (l. to r.): Taylor and Rachel Joiner, Joe Bidewell, Derek Wolfe, Mason Vickery, Casey Sanders, Matt Moody, Andy Willhite, D. Striker, Megan Morrison, Troy Daugherty, and Michael Enwright.*

LEFT: *Jon Koonce, September 1980, backstage at the Euphoria Tavern, Portland, Oregon. Eighteen months later, his band, Johnny and the Distractions, sold out the Portland Paramount Theater one weekend night, and the Seattle Paramount the next. Photograph by David Wilds.* **BELOW:** *Songwriter Hayes Carll in Austin, Texas. Photograph by John Carrico.*

ABOVE: *O'Death at the Bowery Ballroom, New York City, April 5, 2007. Photograph by Jacob Blickenstaff.* **RIGHT:** *Tift Merritt's first of many shoots with photographer Michael Traister, Chapel Hill, North Carolina, 1996. "She was playing her dad's old guitar and worried that he would be upset that it was missing a string in the photo."* **NEXT PAGE:** *Pieta Brown in Iowa City, Iowa, September 18, 2001. Photograph by Sandra L. Dyas.* **LAST PAGE:** *Justin Townes Earle, at home in Nashville, Tennessee, 2007. Photograph by Deone Jahnke.*

In the hands of the Infamous Stringdusters, bluegrass music

this year's
model

may never be the same

by Jewly Hight
photographs by Andrew Rogers

Witness the potential of an Infamous Stringdusters song: "Well, Well" kicks off with a punchy beeline of a groove, Jesse Cobb's mandolin and Travis Book's upright bass darting at sharp angles, heading anywhere but due south. Then — with no apparent warning — they fall into perfect alignment, producing that solid, familiar sound of quarter-notes on bass locked in with a chopping mandolin backbeat.

It's a bait-and-switch on newgrass and bluegrass traditionalists alike.

The audacity.

In truth, the Stringdusters' aim for the song — it's on their self-titled second album and a fixture in live sets — isn't as sinister as all that, but they certainly intend it to prick ears. The way that dobro player and singer Andy Hall talks about it (he wrote the song and sings lead on it), jumping tracks and doing something different every once in a while is necessary. "It's good to try and break up the feel of songs as opposed to just always having one feel," he explains. "You can definitely go back and forth between those two. That funky half-time thing and the bluegrass groove, you can interchange them. Tastefully, hopefully."

Andy Hall

Hall pauses for a moment. "A funky groove isn't unfamiliar to anybody here, even though we all kind of play bluegrassy-type music," he adds.

And that's not an insignificant observation to make about a bluegrass band.

The six-strong Stringdusters — Hall, Book (who also handles some vocal leads), Cobb, fiddler and singer Jeremy Garrett, banjo player Chris Pandolfi, and guitarist Andy Falco (the most recent addition to the band) — think nothing of bringing their myriad influences into play. Folk, jazz, blues, rock, fusion, whatever: It all comes head-to-head with a traditional bluegrass sound, while keeping the distinctiveness of bluegrass intact, at least to some degree.

Tim O'Brien, himself known for being a shape-shifter in acoustic music, knows their approach to musical synthesis firsthand, as he co-produced the new album with the band. "That's part of who they are," he ventures. "They're younger guys. They didn't grow up in the country, most of them. It's today's model of bluegrass bands. They're just doing what they do."

Today's model, indeed.

That may sound like a designation better fitted to a new refrigerator (or an MP3 player) with a sleek, revamped design and a long list of bells and whistles, but it works just as well when

---

Overleaf: The Infamous Stringdusters at the Ark in Ann Arbor, Michigan, July 2008 (l. to r.): Andy Falco, Jesse Cobb, Travis Book, Jeremy Garrett, Andy Hall, and Chris Pandolfi.

looked so cool." — *Jesse Cobb*

you apply it to the Stringdusters. These hot young pickers (all between the ages of 27 and 35, though nobody will say who's at the high end of that continuum) are no bluegrass purists. Nor do they aspire to be, as Pandolfi makes amply clear: "For us, bluegrass is only a small part of that influence pool. I don't listen to bluegrass as much as I listen to other stuff right now. I've gone through periods where I did. I think that's how you should be if you want to do something different."

And they surely do something different for a bluegrass band.

As a formal unit, the Stringdusters arrived on the scene not all that long ago. The founding members bowed out of sideman gigs with the likes of Ronnie Bowman (Hall, Cobb and Garrett all played in Bowman's band), Drew Emmitt (Pandolfi) and Dolly Parton (another gig of Hall's) to launch the band full-time in 2005. They released their first album, *Fork In The Road*, in 2007; it tied J.D. Crowe's *Lefty's Old Guitar* for IBMA Album of the Year, no small feat for a debut. Their second album came out this past June.

Jeremy Garrett

In bluegrass lineage, they're preceded by multiple generations of folks who've forged and tinkered with sounds. Some of the more recent trailblazers — all-terrain banjo master Bela Fleck comes to mind — are musical omnivores who've worked up rather far-ranging incarnations of stylistic fusion. And to the Stringdusters, *everything* that came before them — Bill Monroe, the Grateful Dead, and the Flecktones included — is part of the progression of acoustic music and, therefore, appropriate for their present-day inspiration. "Our idea of bluegrass is very different from a lot of other folks," allows Hall.

"They draw on the whole history of it, including right up to yesterday, which is kind of cool," O'Brien observes. "Their overview is rare."

That the Stringdusters don't feel beholden to any strict notion of tradition has something to do with what late bloomers most of them were in discovering acoustic music. Only Garrett and Cobb were thoroughly immersed in the music early on.

Garrett first picked up the fiddle (violin, really) with the Suzuki classical method at age 3, and his dad, Glen Garrett — a former president of the Idaho Bluegrass Association — got him listening to Flatt & Scruggs. "I had other musical influences, but I studied bluegrass like it was the ultimate music," Jeremy remembers. Father and son played in a four-piece bluegrass band in Idaho called the Grasshoppers, and recorded a traditional bluegrass gospel album together, rife with shape-note-schooled close-harmony singing, in 2005.

Cobb started playing around the start of his teenage years, after he found a string-less mandolin lying around the house. He convinced his folks to buy some strings for it when he learned chord fingerings without the strings. "We didn't have much money, so buying a set of strings was like, 'Well, you've got to show that you're going to be into it,'" he explains. Then his family got a band going, the Cobb Brothers: "We sounded as close to New Grass Revival as we possibly could. We covered New Grass Revival songs. We dressed like them. I wanted to get a perm because I thought Sam Bush's hair looked so cool." (His dad wouldn't let him.)

The other Stringdusters traveled more roundabout routes. Explains Hall, "Me and Andy [Falco], Travis, Panda [Pandolfi], we started out listening to modern music. I mean, rock 'n' roll, you look back and it comes from blues and country and bluegrass. So we just kind of worked our way back." Hall even claims to have been the beneficiary of a Black Sabbath-and-bluegrass link.

"I used to play shred guitar stuff," he reveals. "I think there was an element of young-guy testosterone that bridged the gap between heavy metal and bluegrass.

"It sounds ridiculous, but I honestly feel like the hot picking element, I was into that [same] sort of thing, just in a different style. When I heard the picking in bluegrass, I was like, 'Man, this is just as cool, if not cooler [than metal].'"

All of that, plus formal musical education at Berklee College of Music (where tendonitis forced Hall to switch from guitar to dobro, and where Pandolfi was the first ever banjo principal, though they weren't there at the same time) and at South Plains College in Texas (where Garrett studied in the Bluegrass and Country Music program), contributes to the Stringdusters' broad musical perspective.

As variously attuned as they are, their music is potent and focused. It leans on bluegrass as a foundation more explicitly and consistently than did New Grass Revival through the '70s and '80s (it traffics in a variety of grooves and instrumental ideas, but no reggae, rock vocals or electric instruments to speak of), and more than Nickel Creek has since their first album (it's not as abstract or steeped in alt-rock as that now-on-hiatus trio

Chris Pandolfi

can be). But the Stringdusters also have something hip and youthful about them — call it a wider awareness which transcends bluegrass — that Nickel Creek also shares. As the back-and-forth shifts in groove during "Well, Well" suggest, the Stringdusters have struck their own sense of musical balance between tradition and variation. "I don't think that we concentrate on keeping one foot in tradition or anything," Cobb offers by way of demystification. "I just like it."

Pandolfi talks about bluegrass tradition like he's both ambivalent about it — namely the way well-established material can take precedent over new compositions — and can't tear himself away from it (particularly Earl Scruggs-style banjo playing). "When I say that bluegrass is homogenized," he explains, "a lot of that has to do with material. You hear a lot of the same stuff over and over, and as that canon gets established, so does the feel that goes along with it. But

the gap between heavy metal and bluegrass." — *Andy Hall*

there are things in there that I love. When it comes to Scruggs' playing, the thing that is particularly astounding is timing."

"Since I've learned the Scruggs stuff," he continues, "it's helped me to put some of the more out-there ideas that I developed early on in my playing in context and give them a foundation from which to jump out, instead of having all these crazy ideas be the bedrock of my playing."

Since Pandolfi and most of his bandmates encountered varying forms of experimentation before they really grabbed hold of the basics, they're seldom out to preserve tradition simply for its own sake. Pure nostalgia isn't even on the radar.

When it comes to making albums, for example, the Stringdusters don't do traditional numbers. At least, they haven't yet. To them, the whole point of recording is to create a vibrant, original body of work that gives them space to use their unique voices — singing, songwriting, instrumental. There may be six of them, no small band by bluegrass standards, but they're all hot, dynamic players, and together they have a sound with a great deal of range and depth, moving between straight bluegrass drive, funkier pulses and expansive instrumental work.

Jesse Cobb (l.) and Travis Book

Pandolfi's banjo rolls incorporate jazz-tinged melodies, Hall's dobro work is fiery and stately in turns, and Garrett's fiddling cuts through with sharp, blue strokes. As "Well, Well" proves, Book is a nimble bassist, capable of doing much more than straight timekeeping, and Cobb's playing bears a resemblance to Bush's funky subdivision of beats. "This band, for everybody, it kind of opens up little places to do the things that we've always wanted to do and you can't really do in a traditional bluegrass band," Cobb relates. "So I'm lucky these guys let me do some of that."

Falco, formerly a Mike Bloomfield-influenced electric blues guitarist, often contributes bursts of blues attack. "There are definitely moments in the show that I am approaching the acoustic guitar exactly as I would if we were playing electric," he says, "and you can't do that in most acoustic bands." It's not just his playing that he's talking about, but also the way he can get caught up in the music bodily, from head to toe.

The Stringdusters are all respectable songwriters, some of them (Falco, Hall and Pandolfi, specifically) prolific enough that they need solo albums to catch the overflow. Hall's "My Destination" and Garrett's "Dream You Back" mark some of the band's best writing on *Fork In The Road*, both surprisingly buoyant for bluesy songs about losing love. The new album holds more in the way of quality ballads (Book's "Bound For Tennessee" and Hall's "The Way I See You Now") and

"For us, bluegrass is only a small part of that influence pool." — *Chris Pandolfi*

adventurous yet accessible instrumentals (Pandolfi's brightly melodic "Glass Elevator," Cobb's lighthearted "Golden Ticket," and Hall's fast and muscular "Black Rock"). Falco joined just before work started on the album, so none of his compositions appear, but it's likely that will change in the future.

Whatever songs they don't write themselves, they generally draw from contemporary songwriters like John Pennell, Sarah Siskind, and Bad Livers leader Danny Barnes. (The Stringdusters have fashioned "Get It While You Can," from Barnes' *Dirt On The Angel* album, into one of their most rubbery, laid-back and funky moments). Siskind, now Book's fiancée, is the writer of the bruised, emotionally deep "Lovin' You," which during shows is a regular launching pad for some of the band's most frenetic solos.

Live, their song selections are more varied. They might throw in a traditional number or two, such as the Stanley Brothers' "Lonesome River" or "Weary Heart." "We find that when we play to a more traditional audience, if you play one traditional bluegrass song done a very authentic way, it allows the crowd to enjoy the more out-there things that you do," Pandolfi reasons. "It could just be as simple as you show them that you can do that thing and you have a respect for that, and that opens a big door.

"It's just as much because that's a strong foundation for the band," he adds. "That's really the common thread between us all, is bluegrass. We all have a wide variety of influences and backgrounds musically, but the one thing that we have distinctly in common is bluegrass."

Like most forms of roots music, bluegrass long ago ceased to be confined to a geographic region. Japan has its own bluegrass groups now. Still, it was no further back than 2006 when Rhonda Vincent felt the need to argue, sweetly enough, that being from Missouri didn't undercut her bluegrass authenticity in her song "All American Bluegrass Girl." Region doesn't mean what it once did, but — for better or for worse — it still can connote a little something in terms of signaling insider/outsider identity.

Not one of the Stringdusters is from the south, the traditional cradle of bluegrass, though they've all relocated to Nashville in recent years. Falco, Hall and Pandolfi are from New York state, Garrett is from Idaho, Cobb is from Wisconsin, and Book — the last to give up what he calls his "ski bum lifestyle" and move to Tennessee — is from Colorado. Hall and Pandolfi (along with founding member and original guitarist Chris "Critter" Eldridge, who left in 2007 to join Chris Thile's Punch Brothers) first began their conversations about starting a like-minded original band in Boston.

So the Stringdusters — geographic mutt of a group that they are — don't have much in the way of distinct regional markings. Book's warm, grainy singing (his is the least traditional bluegrass voice in the group) has no trace of an accent. The pinched intensity of traditional bluegrass singing is most evident in Garrett's emotional voice; Hall's clear, reedy singing falls somewhere between. But they're still a ways away from hardcore twang.

Besides, most of their song lyrics aren't bound to any particular time or place. Even the modal, Civil War-themed march "Three Days In July," on their second album, imagines a setting in Pennsylvania, not the south.

That the Stringdusters aren't stamped by region affects to some degree the way they're heard by audiences, traditional or non, and it may make their music more approachable for the latter. "Some people don't take them as authentic as a result," O'Brien notes. "I think, in the long run, they're just being themselves. They're just working through this genre which eclipsed a region a long time ago."

Talk with the Stringdusters for any length of time and you notice not only their musical intelligence, but also how tech and business savvy they are. By and large, those aren't exactly things bluegrass bands have been particularly known for. "Usually you get somebody that's really good with the business, but they don't play as well or you get vice versa," says O'Brien. "In this band, it's all there."

Pandolfi talks about things like cross-promotional opportunities and how the Stringdusters seize every chance to add rock clubs to the more traditional bluegrass venues and festivals they

play. "Bluegrass is popular," he explains, "but we want to strike out and play to younger crowds, and the more diversity you have, the more sustainable your whole operation is."

That's yet another way the Stringdusters embody a new model for a bluegrass band: They want to take their music — same set list and everything — into rock clubs and play it for twentysomething audiences. They're starting to do it, too, and not just because twentysomethings can see themselves reflected in the young, not-too-serious, casually-dressed band, though no doubt that's part of it. But also, the band's way

Andy Falco

of combining virtuosic musicianship with their efforts to redefine what bluegrass is to them now, in light of all the music that's been made up to this point, inspires close listening among older and younger audiences alike, and for different reasons.

"One thing that most of our fans have in common is that they all like to listen to what we're doing, which I know sounds silly," Hall says. "You'd think anyone who goes to a concert is there to listen, but that's definitely not the case."

Pandolfi shot and edited video footage of the band's recent European tour, documenting, among other things, various members engaged in backstage "sword fights," heralded by ceremonial blasts from a toilet plunger "trumpet." Those clips are posted online for anybody to see, and they underscore what the Stringdusters well know — that their individual and collective personalities, in part, make the band what it is.

"The [inner-band] relationship thing, that's the X-factor," says Pandolfi. "That's sort of

which is kind of cool." — *Tim O'Brien*

what brings it all to life, whereas those other elements [songwriting and musicianship], I think you could see those on paper and they would mean something. But the relationships, that's the unique thing about the band that you can't really replicate otherwise."

Says Book, "We take the music seriously. We really care about it, and we take the songwriting seriously. But at the end of the day, the most important thing is that you're enjoying it and having a good time. It makes it easier to enjoy it when the shows are full and people are digging the music and you're playing good music and you can actually play your instrument. But that's the end goal — just to enjoy it."

For the Stringdusters, goofy camaraderie is no marketing ploy. They enjoy hanging out together even when rehearsing, touring and recording don't require it. Referring to the recruitment of Falco when Eldridge left the band last year, Hall notes that "we're not a band where we needed somebody, so we just went and got whoever. It was as much about the hang and the friendship as anything."

That relational energy animates their playing, especially live. If they're not tethered to a microphone, one or two or three of them will often cross the stage, circle up and dig in, egging on each other's soloing with smiles and nods.

"They've got their own little insider language, both musically and cracking jokes," O'Brien says. "They're a happy band. They really are enjoying what they're doing. It shows in the music. It's just kind of joyous, bubbly stuff. They're excited about it."

That they're excited about it — *and* good at what they do *and* original-sounding *and* going about it in their own way — makes them exciting to hear.

Much of that excitement traces back to the Stringdusters having primed themselves for taking bluegrass in a new direction with their varied musical touchstones. Plenty on Pandolfi's lists of favorite groundbreakers are outside the bluegrass canon: "Zappa. The Flecktones fall squarely into that category. I started going to see Bela, and then I got a banjo, and I had never really heard of bluegrass."

A veteran of acoustic bands, Falco realizes the Stringdusters' open-eared philosophy isn't something to take for granted. "You never lose your sensibilities of what you grew up playing," he says, "and what I love about this band is that I'm actually able, for the first time ever, to sort of tap into different areas of where I learned how to play, and bring it in."

Jewly Hight lives and writes in Nashville, Tennessee. She is at work on a book about spirituality and women songwriters.

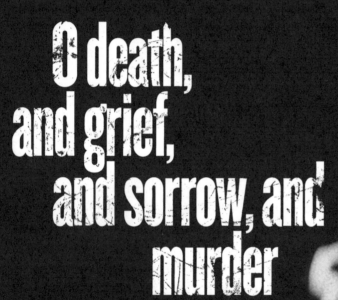

O death, and grief, and sorrow, and murder

In the hands and strings and voice of Crooked Still, the old songs are haunting but not necessarily ominous

by Lloyd Sachs
photograph by David Wilds

We have been here quite a bit lately on this cold, cold ground, courtesy of the young string bands and other roots artists working the graveyard shift. Songs of vengeance and remorse, death and redemption from the pre-bluegrass era are coming back to us in regular doses, spiffed up but still spooky, respectful but not reverent. On *Still Crooked*, the third album by Boston's Crooked Still, people get "stabbed in the heart" and "thrown on the ground." They get laid to rest in a "bed in the snow" and spend eternity "where the wild wildflowers grow." Just for topographical variety, one unfortunate soul gets "drowned in this ocean dear," and then there's the poor guy who gets a glimpse of his sorry fate when he asks his baby to "Please bake me some bread," having pointedly asked her who's been "fishing in my pond." His baby's response: "Johnny, I'd rather see you dead!"

Listening to *Still Crooked*, with its songs of ancient origin and unknown authorship, you can practically hear moths nibbling through the yellowed music. A dark fog covers the ground. But even as history asserts itself, equal parts grim and romantic, the airy, offbeat arrangements — featuring banjo, cello, double bass and fiddle — keep things light and lively. As Aoife O'Donovan's cool vocals curl around the words like mentholated smoke or float over them, feather-like, you may be caught up or even a bit put off by the disconnect between the ghosts who passed down these songs from across the sea, and over the Mason-Dixon Line, and the bright, conservatory-schooled players who are putting their own spin on them.

It was one thing when young Bob Dylan dove into these waters and climbed these hills. Then, as now, Dylan both defied and defined time in absorbing songs from the past — from "another country," as Greil Marcus termed it in *Invisible Republic*. But Dylan was/is Dylan. Crooked Still are mortal. When the band was formed in 2001, its members' ages showed: O'Donovan was all of 18. Banjo player Greg Liszt, cellist Rushad Eggleston and bassist Corey DiMario weren't much older. And now, following the recent exit of Eggleston to make what one colleague called "strange rock" in Los Angeles, and the drafting of cellist Tristan Clarridge and fiddler Brittany Haas, Crooked Still is even younger, and more mortal. The new recruits have barely dipped their toes in their 20s.

Well, so what, you say. Stevie Winwood was 16 when he had people thinking he was a seasoned blues singer (and a black one to boot) on "Gimme Some Lovin'." Drummer Tony Williams was a precocious 17 when he drove Miles Davis' immortal '60s quintet. And how old were the Beatles when they emerged from Liverpool as American roots devotees? Age, like art, is what you make of it. "The dislocation gives the songs a certain mystique," says Liszt. "It heightens the mystery."

All things being cyclical, there's nothing unusual about the interest so many contemporary artists are investing in pre-bluegrass, pre-country and pre-swing — artists including not only string bands and folkies, but also pop group the Decemberists, with their Old World seafaring sagas and murder ballads; instrumental artist Bill Frisell, with his resonant investigations of compelling figures such as Dock Boggs and Roscoe Holcombe; and of course Californian-gone-

---

Crooked Still (overleaf) onstage at the Basement in Nashville, Tennessee, July 2008. They are (l. to r.): Greg Liszt, Aoife O'Donovan, Corey CiMario, Brittany Haas, and Tristan Clarridge.

"What I really love about traditional music — Irish, gypsy, American roots, whatever

Appalachian singer and songwriter Gillian Welch. Still, you have to wonder what about life in these 2000s is inspiring such attractions and connections.

For young Dylan, all roads led to civil rights (his 1963 song "Oxford Town," revived on Crooked Still's 2006 album *Shaken By A Low Sound*, was inspired by James Meredith's travails as the first black student to enroll at the University of Mississippi). Are the old songs, with their lurid death scenarios and grievous laments, now embraced as vehicles to escape the desensitization of an era in which casualties of war are reduced to numbers and kept off-camera, and to rescue rampant violence and other sordid realities from mundanity? Or are the old songs just cool sounding, with their spooky chords and scales and ungussied expression?

"Most of those old recordings were made by people who were learning to play," said Eric

Crooked Still at Merlefest, 2007 (l. to r.): Rushad Eggleston, Corey DiMario, Aoife O'Donovan, and Greg Liszt.

Merrill, the fiddler and old-time music maven who produced *Still Crooked*. "No one seemed to know yet what a record should be. There were different ways of putting one together. The music reflects that openness. Two people will listen to one of those pieces and have a radically different sense of what the song is." Witness O'Donovan's cool, de-bluesified take on Robert Johnson's "Come On In My Kitchen" (a highlight of *Shaken By A Low Sound*), which couldn't be more different from Cassandra Wilson's earthier, more darkly intense reading on 1993's *Blue Light Til Dawn*.

Ultimately, Crooked Still was drawn to the material by both its substance and its style. "What I really love about traditional music — Irish, gypsy, American roots, whatever — is how it exists in context with what's come before," DiMario says. "It's about real people, going through stuff, who needed music to survive. I'm more moved by a scratchy field recording, out of tune and with rough edges, than anything modern. The emotional content underneath resonates with deeper meaning."

On the new album, its third on the Signature Sounds label, Crooked Still steps away from the footloose effects of the band's 2004 debut *Hop High* and the hard-edged chamber approach of *Shaken By A Low Sound* (the latter of which was produced by Frisell's longtime helmsman, Lee Townsend). Altering its temperature and tone without compromising its identity, O'Donovan

— is how it exists in context with what's come before." — Corey DiMario

and company relocate themselves in a spacious, bottom-rich, cerebral sound that evokes bands as disparate as Cowboy Junkies and Blonde Redhead.

Even in the absence of Eggleston, an AC/DC and Metallica head who went for the throat with his slashing solos and created stormy weather with his heavy, percussive sound, it can't have been easy for a band with Crooked Still's chops to *sotto* its *voce*. Liszt, a Bela Fleck devotee, is no shrinking violet with his unusual four-finger attack on banjo and his fondness for hip-hoppish rhythms. And the new edition of Crooked Still had little more than a week to play together and learn the songs for *Still Crooked* before recording them.

That they pulled it off with such ease and such a strong sense of togetherness surprised the founding members. "On our previous records, it was all out, balls to the wall, from start to finish," said O'Donovan, whose first name, a common one in Ireland, is pronounced EE-fa. (She claims she never gets asked about it, but admits to going by Eva in restaurants and hotels to make things easier.) "Now, we're more of an ensemble, more cohesive. It's less about trading solos than serving the songs."

"We wanted to bring out the content of these songs, not to overshadow them," said Liszt.

"You can only exist on pure novelty for so long," said DiMario.

There certainly has been no shortage of novelty, pure or other, in the string-bands that have multiplied in the aftermath of *O Brother, Where Are Thou?*

PHOTOGRAPH BY DAVID WILDS

Crooked Still at the Basement, July 2008 (l. to r.): Tristan Clarridge, Brittany Haas, Aoife O'Donovan, Corey DiMario, and Greg Liszt.

and the breakthrough success of Alison Krauss & Union Station. This well-documented movement has included such groups as Nickel Creek, the Duhks, the Mammals, Old Crow Medicine Show, Uncle Earl, and the Carolina Chocolate Drops. But if some musical trends inspire imitative, cookie-cutter approaches, this one has provided an umbrella for diversity. "Listen to four of these bands and you hear four completely different things," says DiMario. "Everyone is trying to find a way to deal with this music in a unique way."

For Crooked Still, that has involved exploiting the absence (most of the time) of guitar. "Instead of playing against chords, fiddle and banjo play against a drone or key center," observes Merrill, who lived with DiMario after moving from Seattle to Boston in the late '90s. "That keeps

"My mother wanted me to stop doing science and start playing

the harmonies moving." Such is this band's gift for restraint that when the strings come together, full sail, to ride those harmonies, you're unprepared for the electrifying, atmospheric power they attain. You can't help wishing that on songs such as the upbeat "Tell Her To Come Back Home" (featuring a harmony vocal by Tim O'Brien, one of several name contributors on these albums), Crooked Still allowed themselves the luxury of stretching out more. "I love the way the bass and cello fit together and don't get in each other's way," says DiMario. "There's a lot of space for people to do stuff."

As independent-minded as the band is, Crooked Still has no problem being lumped together with the other young acts using bluegrass as a springboard. Belonging to this club has drawn added exposure, and their personal encounters on the festival circuit have led to strong ties. "It's like having a built-in family," says O'Donovan, who, like everyone else in Crooked Still, is involved

in numerous other projects. She and Ruth Ungar Merenda of the Mammals, who appears on all three Crooked Still albums, collaborate in the all-female trio Sometymes Why (which, says its website, is "more aligned with Feist, Joni Mitchell and Bessie Smith than Bill Monroe and the Bluegrass Boys"). The third member of Sometymes Why, Kristin Andreassen, is part of the all-female band Uncle Earl. O'Donovan, who sang with veteran fiddler Darol Anger's Republic Of Strings quintet, also has performed with the jazz-tinged Wayfaring Strangers, which featured Eggleston. Di-

Tristan Clarridge (left) and Brittany Haas onstage with Crooked Still for the first time at Globalfest in New York, January 2008.

Mario is a mainstay of Vermont fiddler Lissa Schneckenburger's band. And around it goes.

O'Donovan's actual family, "a great singing family," whetted her appetite for music of other cultures from the time she was little. Brian O'Donovan, her musician father, hails from West Cork, Ireland, and regularly had leading Irish players over at the house (he hosts the music program "A Celtic Sojourn" on Boston radio station WGBH). Her mother played as well. Aoife stepdanced and, enamored of Ani DiFranco, the Story and the Indigo Girls, formed a musical partnership at age 12 with her friend Sara Heaton (now a rising opera singer). "I was never interested in pop music," she said.

A die-hard New Englander who claims to be a direct descendant of Salem witch trials victim Rebecca Nurse, O'Donovan first started playing with DiMario, a native of central Massa-

the banjo again." — *Greg Liszt*

chusetts, when both were studying jazz and klezmer and other ethnic styles at the New England Conservatory of Music. Eggleston, a California native, was in Boston attending the Berklee College of Music. Liszt, who grew up in Charlottesville, Virginia, "surrounded by bluegrass and folk" but was largely oblivious to it until he took up the banjo at age 15, was at MIT pursuing a doctorate in molecular biology.

"My mother wanted me to stop doing science and start playing the banjo again," said Liszt. He got his Ph.D. and satisfied his mother, director of a modern dance company, after hooking up with O'Donovan, DiMario and Eggleston. And, oh yes, he enjoyed a splashier stroke of good fortune to make his mom proud. A musical acquaintance, Larry Eagle, the drummer in Bruce Springsteen's Seeger Sessions band, called to say they were looking for a banjo player. "I auditioned in Asbury Park," Liszt recalls. "If it hadn't gone further than that, it would have changed my life. But I ended up realizing my childhood fantasy of rocking out with the Boss."

Liszt was on tour with the Sessions band for more than a year, during which his place in Crooked Still was taken by Noam Pikelny, a young (of course) wiz who has played with Leftover Salmon and Chris Thile. Liszt now lives in New York, but with Springsteen having returned to the E Street Band, he's back in Crooked Still full swing.

Any appreciation of the folk and bluegrass scene in New England has to take into account the great Boston folk revival of the 1950s and '60s, when such artists as Joan Baez, Tom Rush, the Jim Kweskin Jug Band (featuring the great Geoff Muldaur and his then-wife Maria Muldaur), Eric Von Schmidt and Peter Rowan held forth. "That scene still has a lot of presence," said DiMario. "Young folk traditionalists are still happening in Boston in a big way." For folkies, Harvard Square's Club Passim, which marks its 50th anniversary this year, was among the key gathering places. For bluegrass players, the Cantab Lounge in Cambridge has become a beloved focal point. Quiet before *O Brother*, it is now a major hot spot through its weekly bluegrass shows. "It did a lot for all our careers," O'Donovan says.

Many singers awakened to the glories of mountain music by T Bone Burnett's *O Brother* soundtrack have honored the past through an austere, plainspoken approach to the songs. In

Aiofe O'Donovan and Greg Liszt onstage at Globalfest in New York, January 2008.

PHOTOGRAPHS BY JACOB BLICKENSTAFF

bringing to this deep body of work their rockish energy and modern cool, Crooked Still was not aiming to "bring young listeners to bluegrass," as one rote analysis claims. "I don't have passion for bluegrass," said O'Donovan. "I have passion for music."

Music that takes many turns. "You won't find any straight-up waltzes from us," she says with a laugh. But otherwise, you never know what Crooked Still is going to do, having lowered funky riffs on Bill Monroe's "Can't You Hear Me Callin'"; double-timed Dylan's "Oxford Town" and merged it with the traditional tune "Cumberland Gap"; toughened and intensified Welch's "Orphan Girl"; and, on the new album, brought an almost disconcerting cheeriness to that "Johnny, I'd rather see you dead" song, Mississippi John Hurt's "Baby What's Wrong With You."

For *Still Crooked*, Merrill had the band listen to 50 rarities drawn from field recordings, reissues of 78s and other sources (including websites such as Kentucky's Berea College Appalachian Sound Archives, which specializes in fiddle and banjo tunes). "For me, the best material is old and strange," Merrill says. "I set out to find songs that are old and of unusual character, but still fit into a modern framework. Modal ballads with seventeen verses are of no interest to me." Neither, for the most part, are songs from the British Isles — until they get imported to and enriched in America.

"We were mainly looking for a good melody, great lyrics, that could lend themselves to a Crooked Still treatment," said O'Donovan. "Some of the songs jumped out at us, like Ola Belle Reed's stunning recording ['Undone In Sorrow']. We just wanted

Crooked Still with Darrell Scott (right) at the Basement in Nashville, Tennessee, July 2008.

to do it." Other songs made the cut after the band stripped them down and tried them on for size. "Low Down And Dirty," O'Donovan's first original for Crooked Still, was based on the legendary Virginia fiddler Hobart Smith's "Graveyard Blues."

(In cases where the authorship of a song isn't known — and some of these things go back hundreds of years — Crooked Still credits the singer or singers they learned the tune from. "The Absentee," for example, is "From the singing and playing of Mr. and Mrs. Sams," a back-porch North Carolina duo of eccentric rough edges. "The recording starts out with Mrs. Sams singing a cappella about Sunday School and whatnot," writes the band in its song notes. "About halfway through the recording, Mr. Sams comes in on the loudest guitar you've ever heard. I think Brittany literally jumped out of her seat.")

and strange."   — *Eric Merrill*

Still Crooked was recorded at Allaire Studios in Shokan, New York, not far from Woodstock, in a bare, open room. Its calm intimacy played an important role according to Merrill. Though Liszt says the band "made a conscious effort to come up with a coherent group of songs," they made no conscious effort to change their approach with the two new players.

"Things took on a life of their own, flowing from their personalities," said DiMario. "Tristan and Brittany are formidable musicians. They had a lot of great ideas. We wanted them to feel like they were part of the band, not replacements. We had always had fiddlers as guests [Haas played on *Hop High* as a teenager] and wrote arrangements with that in mind."

"Tristan and Brittany brought a lot of grace to the music, and such innate musicality," said O'Donovan. "Their strings really enhance the beauty of the old songs. Even if you hear them for only for ten seconds, they push things to a different place."

For the new members, gravitating to the distinctive emotional weather of Crooked Still may well have been more challenging than mastering the arrangements, particularly as they serve O'Donovan. With all of her star quality, she holds back, never allows herself the luxury of ruffling the surface. The emotions in the songs come to her. There can be such an enigmatic quality to her vocals that when she's in a lighthearted mode — as on "Poor Ellen Smith," a jaunty tune about the murder of a bad girl — she makes you look past the flippancy in search of a darker truth.

Which brings us, belatedly, to the issue of humor. We moderns may think we have a lock on irony, but songs have always been as much about finding relief from hardship as documenting grave conditions and circumstances. Eerie tunings aside, what sounds spooky and otherwordly to us now in the old tunes, several generations removed, likely sounded familiar and very much of-the-world to the people who brought the songs into being or passed them down. Which is to say there was no shortage of dark comic relief in them.

Ultimately, *Still Crooked* leaves you wondering how the singers and songwriters from those bygone eras would respond to the modern embodiments of their work. The new versions would certainly seem like they were from a different world, but would they sound spooky in reverse? And what of people who listen to *Still Crooked* 100 or 200 years from now? Will they hear otherwordliness in the songs? And will Dylan, long dead and gone, still be Dylan?

For Crooked Still and the rest of us, it's a story to be continued.

When he was in high school in Jericho, Long Island, that blues hotbed, ND *contributing editor Lloyd Sachs turned down an invitation to hear Son House perform "Death Letter" and other killing classics in his friend's living room. He has been haunted by that boneheaded choice ever since.*

Abigail Washburn & the Sparrow Quartet are melding styles and traditions, but it's not world music.

They're simply playing it around the world.

MODERN SOUNDS in BLUEGRASS & EASTERN MUSIC

by **BARRY MAZOR**   photographs by **DEONE JAHNKE**

And so it continues — the conversation about the power and uses of American roots music in our lives and across popular culture. This music, identifiable by its connections in time and place, has, of course, had a flavorful regional or even local past — homemade, and with ambitions to reach about as far as the nearest porch, place of worship, dancehall or saloon. Though hand-me-down, it was most often a direct expression of the people who made it.

American roots music has gone on into a particular, powerful second phase — "present" — for a good long time now. Furthered by those who've blended the music's core tones and themes into commercial American pop (whether called by that name or some other), it's been marketed to a mass, tech-connected audience (you and me both) — an audience safely assumed at first to be American, and then, casting more broadly, at least "western." Country music, roots-rock, all that, has, in its own way, been a reflection of the background, the broader ambitions, and the read on the audience of the people and institutions who've made it.

In 2008, there are still artists looking to the music's future, in action, taking it places — geographic and sonic — unimaginable to players back there on the porch, or even by the original creators of "The Ed Sullivan Show," the *Billboard* category charts, or cable's MTV or CMT. Yet there is no reason to believe that this emerging roots music of a changing America in a more interconnected world will, in the hands of talents who fit the moment, be any less an expression of its makers' aspirations and very identities than at the beginning. Biography, fired by imagination and skill, still looks like musical destiny — only these days, the evidence for it can show up in formerly unlikely places.

For example, there was a moment onstage in Beijing (yes, Beijing) in late 2006 when two members of an American band, clawhammer banjoist and vocalist Abigail Washburn and cellist Ben Sollee, broke into a spontaneous dance. Maybe it was because it was Washburn's birthday. Béla Fleck and Casey Driessen accompanied them on banjo and fiddle. For those who worry about such things, this dance could not be easily classified, or labeled, or pinned in time; but it *might* be described as a celebratory, post-clogging, freeform jitterbug with selective moves adapted from classical ballet. (Apparently Ben had once had some classical dance training.)

The enthusiastic and responsive Chinese crowd, there's little doubt, saw it simply as enticing, wild and free American dancing. And they were correct, but the cultural go-betweens making music there (and momentarily dancing too) were not simply serving as exemplars of some American folk form, or music and dance appreciation advocates. They were in the midst of a contemporary show that challenges some long-lived ideas about roots music limits and directions, reaching out to that Transpacific audience.

"Exactly!" Abigail recalls. "It points to an important part of what we do, really. We are doing this from a completely modern point of view. I know that I'm not trying to re-create *anything*. I did make the point there that it was related to a traditional form of American dance, something called 'clogging,' but I was pretty focused then on being educational as to what they were seeing and listening to. As time's gone on, I've realized that what's probably more important

Abigail Washburn (at right) & the Sparrow Quartet (l. to r.: Ben Sollee, Casey Driessen, Béla Fleck, and Washburn) photographed at the Lake Superior Big Top Chautauqua, Washburn, Wisconsin, July 10, 2008.

"It was the right friends with the right musical minds and adventuresome spirit —

than that is creating a really entertaining and magnetic show. I'm a performer."

The four strong personalities on that far-off stage had only recently meshed into a working, continuing band, and dubbed themselves the Sparrow Quartet — or, as their self-titled, utterly original, and often quite beautiful new album on Nettwerk Records has it, *Abigail Washburn & The Sparrow Quartet*. The name of the group may, for some, recall the New Testament-referencing gospel standard "His Eye Is On The Sparrow." It must for them, too; they recorded that song on their first release, a 2006 introductory EP.

The Quartet's new one, their first full-length release, is the sort of roots-music/Americana recording that begins with an "Overture" which previews and encompasses the many tones that lie ahead. Those tones prove to include American country and folk with hints of bluegrass, jazz, gospel and (but of course) string quartet chamber music. It's the sort that occasionally marries American old-time country melodies and harmonies with original lyrics in Mandarin Chinese. And, first things last, it's all by a band, neither accompanied nor augmented by anybody else,

made up of four markedly innovative musicians.

Fiddler Casey Driessen, still under 30 (just barely), trained by legends such as Vassar Clements and Byron Berline as well as the staff of the Berklee College of Music, has appeared on albums by Steve Earle, Robbie Fulks, and Tim O'Brien, and already has received a Grammy nomination for one of his own albums (2006's *3D* on Sugar Hill). Cellist Ben Sollee, classically trained despite his many attempts to avoid it (see also the sidebar profile on page 89), backed the idiosyncratic modern blues innovator Otis Taylor for years, now has an innovative acoustic soul CD of his own, and appeared on Abigail's 2005 solo debut, *Song Of The Traveling Daughter*.

And, of course, Béla Fleck, the veteran in this gang, and producer of the Sparrow Quartet album, is regularly rated by many to be the most innovative living master banjoist who's not Earl Scruggs. He's had that reputation on the five-string, in genres ranging from bluegrass to jazz to classical music, since even before his celebrated stand with New Grass Revival in the 1980s. He met Abigail at a Nashville music scene party after she'd relocated there a few years ago; she passed him a collection of songs she was working on. ("I listened to it on the way home from the party," Béla recalls, "and I got pulled over for a traffic ticket. I figured that must mean it was pretty good!") Soon after, the two of them were playing banjos together on the all-star 2004 CD *Appalachian Picking Society*, and Béla came along on a Chinese tour by a fledgling, unofficial version of the Quartet.

the right people.." —Abigail Washburn

Yet with all of this talent in the Sparrow Quartet, nobody in the group questions that the group exists because of the sensibility, particular interests, and passions of singer and songwriter Abigail Washburn — referred to by all as "Abby" — and ultimately, because of her story in particular. Many first became aware of her music and multicultural tendencies through her role as a member of the frolicsome, all-female string band Uncle Earl, which has had major festival appearances, an often-televised video, and two CDs on Rounder Records (the second of which, 2007's *Waterloo, Tennessee*, was produced by John Paul Jones of Led Zeppelin). Washburn first met the founders of Uncle Earl at the annual IBMA and Folk Alliance conventions, and on more than one occasion, she has been heard singing Gillian Welch tunes in Chinese as part of an Uncle Earl show. Unusual.

By contrast, the road to the founding of the musical and cultural boundary-busting Sparrow Quartet did not begin in hallways of roots-music get-togethers, but exactly where no one would think to look — with Washburn's early determination to be an international lawyer, a specialist in the settlement of cross-boundary disputes.

"If anywhere between 6 years old and 20, you'd asked me what I wanted to do," Washburn recalled during a pair of interviews for this article, "I would have told you that I wanted to be a judge! I'd sit in court and think philosophically about what's the best way to structure laws to create a framework for how humanity should function. *This* is what I was really interested in; I wasn't thinking of music as an option.

"I wasn't a trained musician; I didn't even play an instrument — though I'd always sung in choirs and backed up little local bands. I majored in philosophy and Chinese Studies in college, and that's where the heart of my passion lay. What really intrigued me was what the role of The Hague [the Dutch home of more than 150 international courts and legal organizations] was going to be in the future, because as we globalize more and more, we're going to figure out that we're not really nation-states, but important cultural groups within a world. I wanted to be a part of *that* discussion."

To fulfill these ambitions, Washburn — who spent much of her childhood in a suburb of Washington, D.C. — was slated to go to law school at Beijing University. During her undergraduate years at Colorado College, she'd spent part of her freshman year in Shanghai, learning Mandarin. She returned to China several times, picking up more of the language and culture and interning for a consulting firm.

She'd also, in the stateside part of her undergrad years, sung gospel songs and Eurythmics tunes with a female a cappella group, befriended the Cleary Brothers bluegrass band, and found that the old-time acts at the occasional bluegrass festival she'd catch held a particular appeal, not least because they seemed more open to female performers. ("The people I was hanging with really felt that bluegrass was for dudes," she noted.) When she heard what Doc Watson could do with clawhammer banjo, and saw how Gillian Welch used the banjo as a singing songwriter, she'd made a mental note that this was the instrument she'd want to grow old with herself, and soon got hold of one. This was already a long way from growing up with a casual relation to music — maybe catching Run-DMC and Salt-N-Pepa on D.C. pop radio.

And then, just as she was leaving for law school, her life changed.

"Maybe spirituality comes into play there," Abby suggests in retrospect, "believing in a destiny that's greater than my own brain can think of. Because I changed course on the drop of a dime. Before leaving for Beijing, I went on this big six-week road trip, with five days of meditating at the very beginning. It was something I'd always wanted to do, because I wondered how monks pull that off, *how* they meditate. Could that enlighten my approach to the world? I was a philosophy major, and I care about that stuff! I was interested in Eastern religion, and in American Buddhism, which is a huge aspect of how Americans see China and Tibet, so I wanted to get a little bit inside of that visceral experience — at an American meditational compound." This compound happened to be situated in that celebrated hotbed of Eastern religion — Louisville, Kentucky. Abigail would head directly from there toward West Virginia, to learn more banjo tunes, and stopped in at IBMA, still set to go to China, but thinking differently.

"What the meditation led me to ask," she remembers, "was, 'Am I doing the right thing with my ability to speak Chinese and my understanding of that culture?' I could communicate well in Chinese, but was I just going to use that to help companies navigate the Chinese market, which I had done, or in contract law? And within a week of that, I was offered a record deal!"

Like everyone else working in modern China, she'd needed to go out at night with business partners to sing karaoke during those early business-oriented stays there. But instead of singing along with some ersatz recorded version of "Ebony And Ivory," as other Americans in these situations were doing, Abigail would bring out her banjo and sing a Chinese translation of something like "Little Birdie," unprecedented for the patrons in those bars to hear — or, for that matter, most anybody in China or anywhere else. In 2004, when she finally did return to the land that so fascinated her, it was on musical tour, along with three other musicians (Casey Driessen being one of them). For a follow-up 2005 China tour, she asked Ben and Béla (both of whom had played on her solo debut) to join her and Casey.

entire show in Chinese." — *Béla Fleck*

"I figured this could be a cool band," Abigail recalled. "It wasn't that I thought it was the perfect instrumentation or anything!" Two banjos, violin, cello — check. But, she says, "It was the right friends with the right musical minds and adventuresome spirit — the right people."

Washburn was, by that point, not only translating old-time American songs into Chinese for audiences of both languages, she was also emceeing shows when over there, and writing her own lyrics in Chinese. "It's quite a thing to see Abigail get in front of a Chinese crowd and emcee the entire show in Chinese," Béla marvels. "They're so shocked by her ability! And it will be interesting to see what happens for her in the future, when she can bring Chinese musicians over here, to a bluegrass festival. We do get to go back and forth between these worlds; it's an awesome opportunity."

Sollee noticed two different sorts of audience responses to those surprising China-friendly elements of the fledgling Quartet's shows. "There was a little bit of novelty in there," he allows, "because we're playing America's country music, as it had been, and this gal was up there singing in Chinese — maybe formal Chinese, but it was still Chinese — and she had big fluffy hair, you know. Actually, I remember people just being astounded by how good Abby's Chinese was. But there were also audiences who were really moved, because Abby writes that original stuff in their own language. Unless you're a great composer or great musician, you don't really write stuff in China. Their folk songs are really old ones that they do in traditional ways. So this was a total statement of individualism, the fact that 'I have an expression, I write a song, and I play it for you.' That's sort of ground-shaking over there. There were quite a few people that were brought to tears by that whole idea."

So the Abigail Washburn who has performed and recorded turns on the old American country "Who's Gonna Shoe Your Pretty Little Foot" and "Ida Red" (the western swing number that was father to Chuck Berry's "Maybelline"), and "Strange Things Are Happening Every Day" (best-known in the Sister Rosetta Tharpe pop gospel version) is also writing 21st-century songs with American roots music sounds and Chinese lyrics. The leap across cultures seems an astounding feat to the many of us not quite so language-adaptable, and it also raises questions about our comfortable ideas of what roots music is, and can be — and about the intentions and ambitions of this artist and this Quartet. Take, for instance, just the seemingly simple matter of placing what we call "old-time" music — often 19th-century or even early 20th-century parlor, dance or pop songs in reality — into a culture that goes back thousands of years. Our concepts and words for "old" and "time" don't translate very well.

"I say that old-time music is the music of the immigrants of America — after they had lived in America for awhile and intermingled," Abby explains. "As for thinking in Chinese, well, if I'm in China, interacting with Chinese people, yes, I do. What happens in that moment is another layer of all this — about how much of me *is* Chinese at this point. I don't know how to measure that exactly, but I can say that everything I do is heavily, heavily influenced by the experiences I've had in China, the really profound love I have for that culture, and how that culture has changed me. Whatever it is in human beings that makes them want to perpetuate a feeling they have or affinity they maintain, I've got that — hardcore.

"We were shooting the moon; we all wanted to make the best record we'd

"The interesting thing is that the multilingual approach is the thing that everybody tells me is going to impede my success — and yet it is the thing that actually draws success to me. And I've been doing it for five years now."

Many have viewed the rhythms of American speech, and southern American speech in particular, as a crucial, perhaps even defining element of why our music sounds as it does. Does having this international, bilingual sensibility and experience shed new light on that, or does it cast doubt on the very notion?

"I'd definitely think that music compensates for speech in rhythm," Abigail responds, "but I would say that this has more to do with cultural custom and nature. In China, some of their most culturally specific art forms, like traditional, pre-western opera, are generally arrhythmic, based on drama and emotion. And it's specific to Chinese music that they look at their natural environment, nature. So many of their traditional compositions are about something like the movement of a butterfly in flight, a sound representation of what seeing that feels like, or it might be what some specific mountain landscape looks like. American music, on the other hand, is really, really connected to a meshing of environment and cultures.

"To me, it's obviously very subjective what 'roots music' is. There is, it's true, a strong reaction to the word 'globalization,' which has to do, in part, with a person's comfort level with transformation. But I want to be clear, in talking about this, that it's really important to me, and to what I'm doing, to retain a very strong sense of where you come from, holding on to what's beautiful about where you already are."

Bela Fleck, a longtime world traveler and musical genre-jumper, actually had less than a full comfort level with Chinese sounds before the Sparrow Quartet experience, which has included much live collaboration with musicians in China and Tibet. "I had some sort of prejudice about it," he admits. "I had played with one Chinese musician, on a record called *Tabula Rasa*, so I actually knew a couple of Chinese tunes from that experience — but I didn't much *like* that sort of thing. But I wanted to open up my head a little bit about that; I had a big hole in my China understanding, so I was curious about it. And we all agreed to go over there. I basically paid my own way to get a vibe on China, figuring it was to be a big player in the future we're living in."

Surely it tells us something about the new state of global pop culture that the Sparrow Quartet has played a club in Beijing called Nashville (a sold-out show), and one in Shanghai called the Cotton Club. They'd also find themselves before audiences outside of the biggest cities in Sichuan province, and before some in Tibet who'd never seen any musicians from beyond their immediate locale at all. The Sparrow Quartet was the first American group to be allowed to play in the beleaguered occupied territory. They played at high schools and colleges, and they opened for the very first Tibet rock band (yes; that's rock band) at a nightclub there. Understandably, Abby found their approach revelatory. "They'll sing something like, 'Oh that girl, she's so pretty; I'll have to ask her older brother if I can date her,' along with a rhythm made with their hands and feet, and then go into a rap — 'Whoa! She's beautiful! It freaks me out!' — and then they go back to the melody," she relates. "And the other thing is, they have that high lone-

ever done." — *Béla Fleck*

some sound in the vocals, like Ralph Stanley or something, really high, but it's not falsetto; it's a strong chest voice."

The China tours, and the unique Tibet swing in particular, marked the point when this band became a band with its own future and potential, and not just a side excursion for all four of them. "It sort of got a motor to it; it really got cookin'," Bela remarks. "With Casey's fiddle added, there were the possibilities with the two bows; that was great for the voice, and it also offset the two banjos. And there was something about it that was just sort of cool! So it was like, 'You know, if we really spent some time on this thing, we could make something we were really proud of."

The resulting *Abigail Washburn & The Sparrow Quartet* disc, described by Abby as "first of all, music that took advantage of everybody's skills, music that we all wanted to play together for a year out on tour," is hardly an unend-ing string of folky American songs in Chinese. Only a notable few of the tunes on the song-oriented collection are in something other than American English, as Abby wrote them; and as for the sounds, well, there's that varied, unique "bluegrass jazz gospel Chinese-American string quartet" factor.

A standout yet typical track is "A Fuller Wine." It's driven by violin and banjo and ripped-to-shards vocal phras-ing, with an imagistic lyric that's at once about both intercontinental and inter-personal relationships. A listener back here in the U.S.A. might not be certain whether it's an adaptation of tones from some western classical music "art song," some Appalachian lick that can't quite be identified, or some utterly unfamiliar Asian traditional sound. You're left without the comforts of a compass or a set of locked definitions, and the important news is that you have no pressing reason to care. It's effectively, persuasively a sound to be taken as it comes to your ear, on its own new terms.

"That's true," Abigail notes, "and that's part of the reason maybe the first listen to our album is not the easiest. I'm *not* saying that our music is not accessible; it's very song-oriented and easy to listen to. But I can see where the second, fourth or 23rd listen get better!…Our whole point was to build compositions around songs with their own meaning, so if anything in the instrumentation might seem too unfamiliar or made people uncomfortable, the answer would be just to listen to the words."

Arriving at this fresh and international synthesis was not necessarily easy. "There were moments where we were totally confused about what to do or how to move forward, or where we had five ideas on what to do with one part," she recalls. "Everybody was extremely intentional about what they were doing on the record, and sometimes we didn't agree. There was a lot of fighting for what we believed in, so I wouldn't say it was a very *fun* process. It was intense! Luckily, most of the personalities were spurred on by the challenge and the debate."

Project producer and veteran arranger Fleck necessarily had a central diplomatic role in those deliberations. "We'd sit around in a circle with the song, and throw ideas around," he explains. "I'd kind of referee, when it was needed, running interference and getting the job done — but that wasn't needed that often, since, generally, everybody worked well together in this case. Sometimes I'd get a blaze of ideas and sort of ram them down people's throats — or somebody else would....It was pretty organic, but there was definitely some unique sense from each of us about what worked and what didn't. We were shooting the moon; we all wanted to make the best record we'd ever done....The challenge was what made it appealing.

"Take Casey, for instance. He's a great bluegrass fiddle player and jammer. But this was new to him, which I think was actually one of the great things about the band for him. He was forced to fit into a different way of playing than he was used to, as great a musician as he already is. He has a tendency to get mangy, rock out, and kick ass; he's got *that* in his back pocket. But here he's being forced to do this real beautiful, soulful stuff, with set parts that can be quite complicated, and to blend with another bowed instrument as part of a string section — all things *he* knew he could do, but nobody else did."

"For me," Béla continues, "the arranging element was the big draw. I love trying to make sense out of things and trying to make something work. It's something I'm pretty good at, taking diverse elements and pushing them into shape until it works. The only real problem that the band *has* is having a lot of music in the same range, because rather than having a bass, there's a cello; rather than a guitar and mandolin, we've got two banjos in the same range. There's a lot of arranging we have to do to keep things from getting cluttered, because when we're all playing full out, there's a roar in the midrange. Sometimes we have to take turns!"

Pickers may well be wondering about how the combining of Bela's audacious, fluid banjo style, ultimately built on the Scruggs-style three-finger roll, with Abigail's older clawhammer style was worked out, since you don't see or hear even *that* every day.

"If you think about it as if they were two guitars, the problem disappears," Bela suggests. "There's the singer-songwriter who wrote the song carrying the groove with that guitar part, and there's the lead guitar player who finds the fills and finds things to do, plays harmony licks. It's just like that, only people are just less used to it."

For the record, Abigail continues on as a working member of Uncle Earl as well, even as the Sparrow Quartet's reach increases, if not at the same time. "I find that I really have to do one thing at a time," she says, "so other than a few appearances with Uncle Earl, we really don't have much on the calendar with that right now — but we will again. One of the reasons that bands break up so often, I think, is that people can't get everything they want out of just one band; it's just so hard. Bela once said to me that a band is a most noble effort, and I agree with him. There are all of these separate, individual lives that have to come together in a band; you spend your

happening fast..."   — *Abigail Washburn*

lives on the road together. If you have more than one project going on, you don't expect so much from any one. It's a lot easier to show elasticity in a group if you have other outlets."

The Quartet was invited by the U.S. State Department to play several shows in Beijing during the 2008 Summer Olympics, and were provided a grant to do so. Such a level of government involvement, as was also the case with China's agreement for them to play in Tibet, provides a partial answer to the reasonable query, "How can a band afford travel like that in this high oil-price/high airfares era?" But it also, unavoidably, raises questions about how Abigail and company view the relation between the musical and cultural exchanges they've been so involved in, and about the international political relations she once saw as the domain for her career. It is, as one could predict, a subject to which Abigail has given considerable thought.

"The American government had never had a conversation with the Chinese government over Tibet, for instance, other than about geo-political issues," she notes. "So this was the first time that another channel was opening up — and it was music, a vibration that could heal through other channels. Instead of just coming into these unending conversations where we all come from basically different orientations and can't agree, this becomes another level to communicate on. The more we can create relationships between Chinese and American people, on a more profound level, the less significance the political conversations will have.

"Look, I'm not expecting a whole lot from people," she adds. "But at the heart of what I'm doing, I do hope that whatever actions I take will have an impact on the world around me. I'm trying to act and create in a way that will help create the world I want to live in. Obviously, I can't control the way people respond, or really predict it....Before I had their language, I just felt like another American tourist in China, and I hated being seen just as some sort of English-speaking robot. It was really frustrating, terrible. Most Americans find that repulsive and then want nothing to do with that society as a result, because it's not all based around them. We really expect services to be built around us — what I want and what I need, and my comfort. And, sure, I'd first felt that way myself. It's one reason that people are in so much pain about globalizing — because they have to change that. The world's not going to revolve around the individual and their dollar bills. I have a really strong notion that at the *cellular* level, globalization is happening fast, and that we're evolving in a way beyond what we're even conscious of."

From the standpoint of a listening experience, the trick — and there's a strong case to be made that the Sparrow Quartet pulls it off — is in creating music that, however far-reaching, is not overtly self-conscious.

"This isn't 'fusion music,'" Abigail says, pointedly. "It's not 'trying to combine two things,' or overlaying a foreign melody over a groove. It's internalization of our global existence right now. I don't even know what 'world music' people talk about is; I think it's a term that's been co-opted by strange marketing forces! Wouldn't it be fun if we could sort of redefine 'world music' as 'the inevitable sounds of internationalization'? What's going on in my music is going on in music all over the world. And 'inevitability' in music" — the notion that the art must move forward, just as it is doing — "is probably the most compelling aspect of it: the feeling that where *it's* going is inevitable."

We'll leave Béla Fleck with the last word about that. "One of the reasons this works so well is that Abby's just very natural about it. She's not putting on airs, not trying to be anything she's not. She loves these songs; she loves singing this music that we're doing, and she makes it her own."

Longtime ND *senior editor Barry Mazor is a frequent contributor to the* Wall Street Journal *on country and pop music. His book* Meeting Jimmie Rodgers: How America's Original Roots Music Hero Changed The Pop Sounds Of A Century *is set to be published by Oxford University Press in April 2009.*

SOLO
SOLLEE
SOUL

by BARRY MAZOR

"There are, you know — *expectations* of us," Sparrow Quartet cellist Ben Sollee says. "You've got Béla, who's worked really hard in the musical world, and people that know Casey's an absolute warhorse on the fiddle, and by now there's an expectation of Abby as a light, folkie singing gal." Expectations of Sollee himself may not be quite so defined yet, but they're rising fast for the 24-year-old musician, singer and songwriter out of Lexington, Kentucky. NPR, for instance, dubbed him one of 2007's "Top Ten Greatest Unknown Artists." As substantial as his contributions to the Sparrow Quartet's CD and sound are, they don't provide the full picture. The near-simultaneous release of his soulfully crooned solo disc *Learning To Bend* makes that very clear.

Thirty Tigers, which released the album, refers to the involving, pointed, seriously *realized* disc as "Rock/Acoustic." Ben himself calls it "contemporary folk, but with a real soul orientation. It's just that the dude on it happens to be playing cello." Said cello, sometimes held up in his hands, gets plucked, and picked, and, from time to time, lays down Memphis soul horn lines. That's not a musical attack with much precedent. "I don't think there *is* a lot of precedent for it," he concurs, "but it's one of those things that happened. I grew up playing cello, and I wanted to make those different sounds on it."

Sollee's parents played and sang R&B around Lexington. His dad an R&B guitar ace, his mother an earthy singer in that mode, so he was raised on Wilson Pickett and Otis Redding. But this was Kentucky; his mom's father was an Appalachian fiddler, banjo player and preacher, with whom the fledgling cellist would play along, picking up country tunes. He was also very much of his '80s-born generation, taken with Michael Jackson (he'd dance and sing along with the hits), Ani DiFranco, Dave Matthews, and Eric Clapton's hit lament "Tears In Heaven."

This was all in the context of learning cello, by classical training, beginning in fourth grade. In high school, Sollee fronted a local band, singing and playing electric cello. When he majored in music in college, the one cello player who meant much to him was the Turtle Island String Quartet's Mark Summer, who plucked the instrument, played bass lines, took solos, and stretched the instrument beyond its usual genre confines. This did not necessarily win fans among Sollee's music instructors. "I was really ornery to my teachers," he laughs now. "I just caused them all kinds of hassle, all along the way. They didn't quite know what to do with this cat who really loved playing, and would play a lot, but wouldn't play the stuff you sent him off to play, who'd show up doing [things] totally out of line with the natural curriculum."

The often stunningly modulated, lyric-targeting mid-to-high soul vocals that Sollee exhibits on *Learning To Bend* tracks such as "How To See The Sun Rise" show an ease that reflects, for one thing, a telling understanding of how the style of a singer such as Sam Cooke really worked. "That just sort of showed up, during my actual adolescence," he recalls. "I liked singing, enjoyed having it part of my performing, so I ended up doing it a lot. I think it's a voice that's been passed down; my grandfather had a sort of mid-high tenor voice, just gorgeous. There's a lot of time when I'll sing something and the way it'll come out will really remind me of him. But then, it really reminds me of my mom, too, who was a mezzo-soprano — same range."

The Cooke connection is made explicit with Sollee's contemporary, pointed updating of Sam's "A Change Is Gonna Come," rendered as an outpouring by a soldier on a never-ending tour in

always changing.”   *— Ben Sollee*

Iraq. Equally political, in a way that's forceful yet somehow gentle, pressing *and* pleading, is his own tune, “A Few Honest Words,” which asks for precisely that from anybody who wants to “lead my country” and “tell me about democracy.”

“As a young person, I'm part of a generation that really has to come up and take the reins in the social-economic stuff that we're inheriting,” Sollee posits. “I feel like I'm a part of a bigger voice for that right now. I shy away from making really, really specific statements; I try to find what it is about what I'm feeling that has a broader understanding. It's not that I'm just pissed off with, say, one politician acting in a certain way; it's that I'm pissed off that it's part of the operating status of a lot of politicians.”

It's not coincidental that Sollee apprenticed through a good part of this decade with the sonically experimental, quite contemporary and outspoken blues singer and songwriter Otis Taylor — the sort of blues singer who'd hire a young cellist. Sollee credits Taylor with some of this notable finesse in being politically pointed without preaching. “I do think I picked some of that up from Otis,” Sollee says. “He'd go right to the sources and stories that he'd heard and read, and find whatever sort of heartstring line or moment there was about it, and just put that on the table. It was like he walked into your room, set down a photograph of a lynching, and just walked out — just left you with it to look at. So there is that element in what I do: I just want to sort of put people there and let them stay there, rather than expounding on what I specifically think should be done.”

Sollee's road to the Sparrow Quartet actually began when Rayna Gellert, Abigail Washburn's fiddle-playing bandmate in Uncle Earl, joined in on an Otis Taylor session and met Ben. One thing led to another. “Musically, Otis taught me about creating a fervor — something that could take people off into another place, using rhythm and an overwhelming sound to do it, almost hoodoo-like,” Sollee says. “He was always after that. I remember him teaching me stuff over the phone: ‘Can ya hear that? Can ya *hear* that?’”

In a live setting, Sollee is something of a performing natural. The cellist who broke into a knowing but freeform dance onstage with Abigail, or who has been known to embark on an all-string, countrified take on Stevie Wonder's “Boogie On Reggae Woman” with Casey Driessen, has enough of the pull toward pop in him that he can speak of wanting to “get up in front of a ton of people and totally move and rock them.”

Abigail says of her bandmate, “I loved him from the first as a human being. There was just a real connection between us, a pathos. When he played his cello on my stuff, I could tell that he was coming from this very empathic, emotional place. He leans so much on the music and the words, and with us, will take himself out of the way a lot of the time; he really does. It's really about what's being communicated in the song. And he's really grown as a compositional person himself.”

With all of the sophisticated musical ideas that Sollee's music often shows, as well as the political questions he raises, this particular twentysomething seemingly can't help but emanate an essentially sunny sense of life. “Well, that was the biggest stomping ground for Otis and me,” Sollee reveals. “I believe in the inherent good in human nature, and Otis always fought me on it. He said there would always be wars, there will always be people killing each other. But I'm comin' from Kentucky, where the weather is always changing.”

.she
is.
Carrie
Rodr

Carrie Rodriguez took a leap of faith toward a new artistic identity,

íguez

by **DON MCLEESE**

photographs by **SARAH WILSON**

underlying image courtesy **MARGARET ELIZABETH ALDEN**

but it's just the latest in a series of big steps that have defined her

"**S**he Ain't Me" isn't the title song of Carrie Rodriguez's new release because it's the catchiest, most melodically irresistible tune on the follow-up to her highly praised solo debut *Seven Angels On A Bicycle*. Though it is that. It isn't the title song because the luminous vocal of the Texas singer-songwriter is the most supple singing performance she's ever recorded, with more of a lilt than a twang. Though it is that, as well.

It isn't the title song because it sounds like pop heaven, with harmonies in the arrangement that have more in common with the bittersweet Bangles than with, say, the rougher-edged Lucinda Williams (a hero to Rodriguez who provides vocal counterpoint on "Mask Of Moses," another standout track).

It's the title track because these three words offer a manifesto. Whatever she was, she is no more. Whatever preconceptions one has about the Austin-to-Brooklyn transplant no longer apply. Classical violin prodigy? *She Ain't Me.* Her father's instrumental sidekick? *She Ain't Me.* Chip Taylor's duet partner, accompanist and musical protégé? *She Ain't Me.* Alt-country vocalist? *She Ain't Me.* Tex-Mex fiddler? *She Ain't Me.* Cantina? Conservatory? *She Ain't Me.*

Not that she rejects any of the experiences and influences which have helped forge her musical identity. But she has shed those skins on an album that sounds less like a sophomore effort than like a fresh start. She has a new producer (Malcolm Burn), new writing partners (Gary Louris and Mary Gauthier among them), and a new set of musicians in the studio. The result is an album where the caterpillar turns into a butterfly.

"As soon as we had that song title I knew I wanted to make it the album title," says Rodriguez, who wrote the song with Semisonic's Dan Wilson (who has also co-written with the Dixie Chicks). "Up until then, I was having a hard time coming up with one. And what I liked most about it is that the album is a departure for me, a lot of new things. I have a feeling it is not going to be what a lot of people were expecting. So I feel that by calling it *She Ain't Me,* it's a warning. *This is not what you think it's gonna be.*"

So consider yourself warned, though music fans who take delight in surprise and feel no need to restrict artists to categorical boxes will be amazed at the transformation. Even so, this isn't the first time that it has been hard to anticipate where Rodriguez will go from where she's been. Where some artists seem to progress in a straight line, her musical development has been more like a series of zig-zag turns.

I know I could never have anticipated this album from the Carrie Rodriguez that I first saw back in the early 1990s, when I was the pop music critic at the *Austin American-Statesman*. She was then an accomplished violinist in her early teens, known mainly in the Austin music community as the daughter of respected singer-songwriter David Rodriguez. A charismatic lawyer-activist for whom a limp from childhood polio never seemed much of a handicap, Rodriguez had decided to turn his full attention to writing and performing his music, much of it politically charged.

His daughter would initially join him onstage for a few songs, and eventually would contribute to the spare musical accompaniment throughout his set. Serious and studious, she seemed to be accompanying her dad as a dutiful daughter rather than seeking attention for herself. Leading a band did not appear to be her destiny.

"At 13 when she first came onstage with me, she was neither eager nor reluctant, just cool, calm and competent," writes David by e-mail from Holland, where he emigrated some 15 years ago and is now a Dutch citizen. "She does have my sense of timing, of where the beat should fall. It's so uncanny. When playing with her, from a musical standpoint, it was like having a double onstage. But I think that's genetic."

Accompanying her father represented a whole different musical world for Carrie, who had begun studying the violin at age 5. Her parents had divorced a year or two earlier. Her mother, the acclaimed painter and visual artist Katy Nail, is a classical music buff who had season tickets to the opera. "It was my decision to start the violin," says Carrie. "They were offering Suzuki violin lessons at my elementary school, as kind of a pilot program. I remember walking down the hall and hearing horribly screechy violins playing 'Twinkle, Twinkle, Little

Star,' and being drawn to that sound and wanting so badly to be a part of that. So I came home and said, 'Mom I want to play the violin.' And after that, she was a huge part of that growing up, coming to all my lessons, taking me to see the opera and the symphony.

"But at the same time I do have memories of my dad playing just for me. I remember him playing me political folk songs at bedtime. One of my favorites was 'Drunken Ira Hayes,'" she says with a laugh. (Peter La Farge's "The Ballad Of Ira Hayes" was popularized by Johnny Cash but was better known in Texas music circles as a live staple of Townes Van Zandt's club sets.)

"Sometimes I would see my dad every other week, sometimes not so often. It wasn't like a super regular part of my life. Actually, when I started playing music with him, that was kind of a way for us to reconnect."

Like so many musically-minded kids growing up in Austin, she'd also had exposure to the rich influence of the city's club scene, well before she began performing with her father. Unlike in other cities, it isn't uncommon to see children accompanying their parents to hear bands in the bars.

"I remember hanging out at Waterloo Ice House watching Uncle Walt's Band when I was probably like 5 years old," she says. "My mother would take me to things like that all the time. I thought Champ was the coolest one in the band, because I had curly hair and he had that Afro."

The trio beloved in Austin comprised Champ Hood (whose fiddle playing as well as his curly hair might have made him a role model for Carrie), singer-songwriter Walter Hyatt, and future country hitmaker David Ball. Like Carrie's music now, the music they made together transcended category. It encompassed pop, folk, country, bluegrass, and even a bit of island lilt.

'Twinkle, Twinkle, Little Star,' and being drawn to that..."   — Carrie Rodriguez

Whatever its formative influence on Carrie, there remained a huge gulf between the music for which Austin remains best-known and the formal, classical instruction of her violin training.

"I was very comfortable performing in the classical world. I would do competitions and did solo things, and that was a comfort zone for me," says Carrie. "But any time I had to improvise or come up with my own part, that was scary. And at the very beginning my dad would write out some melodic lines that I could learn. I just didn't know how to do that. Pretty much all through high school, I probably got better little by little, but even by the time I went away to music school, I was by no means a good improviser."

Higher education presented a fork in the road for Carrie. There was no doubt that her twelve years of violin training and competition had prepared her for music education at the next level, yet where should she go? She had a scholarship offer from Ohio's prestigious Oberlin Conservatory of Music, where she could prepare for a career as a classical violinist, but her club performances with her dad had expanded her comfort zone into a different realm. Even if she wasn't a good improviser, she might want to become one.

"I'd actually wanted to go to Berklee [an equally prestigious music school in Boston that places more emphasis on contemporary styles] before I got into Oberlin, but it seemed like too crazy of a thing to do," she says. "All those years of playing with my dad had given me the bug, a little bit, but I got this great scholarship to Oberlin, where they had really good classical teachers, so I decided to do what I was supposed to do.

"But once I got there, I realized that I'd be slaving away, practicing eight hours, playing the same material. Everyone has to learn the same material — this concerto at this time in your education, and then go on to the next. So you're all playing the same thing, it all sort of sounds the same, and there's a million people who can do it better than I can. And that frustrated me. I found myself sitting in my dorm room listening to Willie Nelson and old Hank Williams songs when I was supposed to be in the practice room playing my Mendelssohn or whatever."

Perhaps the turning point in the musical education of Ms. Rodriguez came with the Cleveland concert of Lyle Lovett, a family friend. He had recorded her father's "Ballad Of The Snow Leopard And The Tanqueray Cowboy" on *Step Inside This House*, a two-disc tribute to Texas songwriters he admired, and had recently attended one of her mother's art exhibitions.

"For whatever reason, he was sort of in touch, and invited me to the show and told me to bring my fiddle," she says. "So I remember playing along with his *Road To Ensenada* album and trying to learn the fiddle parts. He let me sit in during soundcheck, and from my recollection I did a really bad job. I think I was just totally not cool, sounding like a classical musician, and I remember feeling fairly embarrassed about it.

"And then I watched the show, and he had a wonderful fiddle player with him, Andrea Zonn. Watching what she did, it just looked like so much fun and so creative, and I wanted to be able to do what Andrea had done that night. That's when I started making calls and figuring out how to get out of Oberlin and get into Berklee, where I knew they had a more liberal type of education with jazz and improvising skills."

The transfer to Berklee had a profound impact on her life's direction as well as her music. It was there that she met her future husband, jazz saxophonist Javier Vercher (whose playing highlights her *Seven Angels On A Bicycle* solo debut), and where she encountered the influence of other instrumentalists exploring the improvisational possibilities of everything from jazz to bluegrass to music beyond category. A violinist when she arrived at Berklee, she was a fiddler when she graduated.

"I had to move up to New England to learn how to play the fiddle," she says with a laugh, while noting that "growing up in Texas, my violin teacher called it a fiddle from day one, even when I was playing Bach on it."

Yet even with the shift in direction that her musical development took at Berklee, Rodriguez had yet to begin even apprenticing at the sort of artistry which defines *She Ain't Me*. She wasn't writing songs. And she wasn't singing them. She had yet to sing onstage, and after one unfortunate experience, had no intention of ever doing so.

"I actually took a class at Berklee called Singing for Non-Vocalists, because I thought it

Carrie Rodriguez and Chip Taylor.

would be an easy A," she remembers. "And I got a C on my midterm! I was awful! I was so nervous that I forgot all the words to the songs. It was so embarrassing, but that was my only singing experience."

Having left Austin to become a classical violinist, she returned in 2000, following her graduation with honors from Berklee, to become a fiddler in a country band. "I wanted to get a gig with a great songwriter, playing fiddle," she says. "The end." She started backing Brian Gowan, a Nashville-style country singer who had previously been signed to Curb, in a band that played dancehalls throughout Texas on weekends. She worked more of the alternative fringes with Hayseed, including an instore appearance during the 2001 South By Southwest festival that would take her career in a direction no one had anticipated.

One of those who saw her play that day was Chip Taylor, the veteran New York songwriter

The end." — *Carrie Rodriguez*

("Wild Thing," "Angel Of The Morning," the Hollies' "I Can't Let Go") who was re-establishing himself as an alt-country recording artist after supporting himself for decades as a professional gambler. He was looking for a fiddler to accompany him and was hoping to find a female instrumentalist who could provide harmony vocals as well. "I was just hoping she'd be good," Taylor later told a reporter. "And she was great."

"He saw me at South By, got my number and said he wanted me to play fiddle with him," she says. "But even at my very first gig, he put up a microphone, and said, 'I'm just going to have a microphone set up for you, and if you hear a harmony, please help me out.'

"I had never done any harmony singing. None. So I was very shy about it, but little by little I gained more confidence to sing more. And once he started hearing me, he said, 'Wow, I love the way your voice sounds with mine. I want to do a duet.' So he taught me this song he had written for Billy Vera and Judy Clay back in the '60s ['Storybook Children,' co-written with Vera], and that became part of the show. Then he worked up a couple more duets, and within six weeks he was asking me to come up to New York and make a duet album with him."

So the billing changed, with Carrie's quick promotion from supporting musician to duet partner. Less Sonny and Cher or George and Tammy than Porter and Dolly, they made a strikingly odd couple (made odder still by the fact that some thought they *were* a couple, offstage as well). He with his white hair and patrician visage; she so smolderingly dark. He from New York, she from Texas. He some four decades older than she, old enough to be her grandfather.

Yet the music they made together let Rodriguez find her voice and extend her musical comfort zone even further than before. Her mother has said that she had never heard Carrie sing, ever, not even in the car, before the release of the duo's *Let's Leave This Town* in 2002. The next two years saw two more releases, *The Trouble With Humans* and *Red Dog Tracks*, with Carrie bringing more attention and success to Taylor's music than he had experienced as a solo artist — some fresh blood to a veteran act. For Carrie, working with Chip was the seminal experience in her development as a singer-songwriter.

"Obviously I wouldn't be singing right now if it wasn't for Chip," she says. "And I don't think I would be writing songs. That just wasn't part of the plan. But the more I worked with Chip, the more I wanted to be more of a partner in what we were doing. And he was really pushing that also, for me to write, so it *was* more of a partnership. It gave me the bug to keep doing it.

"Some of the most basic things that he taught me were the seriousness of the song and finding the best way to deliver it, whatever that is," she continues. "Even if the song has two chords, he's all about delivering that in an honest way, so that people can feel something, and he's feeling something while he's singing it. At the very beginning when I was singing, my first thoughts were always, 'Am I singing in tune? I must sound awful.' And he would keep having to remind me to just turn my brain off and feel the song. It was crucial. And then the other stuff will fall into place."

The more Carrie progressed, the plainer it became to both of them that she couldn't play second fiddle forever, and that a solo album was the next logical step. Once again, Taylor provided both the impetus and the comfort zone. Taylor and Rodriguez co-produced her 2006 Back Porch Records solo debut *Seven Angels On A Bicycle*; they co-wrote four of the songs, with Taylor contributing seven others on his own. They recruited stellar musicians with whom Rodriguez was familiar, including jazz guitarist Bill Frisell (who had played on *Red Dog Tracks),* multi-instrumentalist Greg Leisz, and Carrie's saxophonist husband Javier Vercher.

"I'm sure the album was probably Chip's idea at first, but I was very excited about it," she says. "He didn't have to push too hard. I wanted to see what else would come out."

The results received widespread acclaim. *Seven Angels On A Bicycle* established Rodriguez as an artist with an identity all her own, with a seductive intimacy to her voice, on material steeped in folk-country roots but with arrangements that let the virtuosity of the players soar. "The approach to making it was more like a jazz group," Rodriguez says, though her singing and her songs ultimately attracted more attention than the instrumental interplay.

By her own admission, *She Ain't Me* (which came out in August on Back Porch/Manhattan) has been a scarier project than her debut, which can be seen in retrospect as a transition between her teaming with Taylor and a solo career, as if she were sticking a toe in the water. Now she has taken the plunge, with no safety net. This time through, there's no Chip. There's comparatively little violin. There is no listing of her husband among the musician credits (though his saxophone does sneak into the mix on the title track and "Mask Of Moses"). And there's more of a pop sheen in the arrangements than Rodriguez, a self-described "folkie," has ever heard applied to her music.

The distance traveled between the two albums is evident from their respective photo sessions, both shot by Sarah Wilson, a childhood friend whose photography has been featured in *Texas Monthly*. The photos for the debut weren't even planned with a cover in mind — just two friends hanging out, Carrie looking and dressing like she might any day in Texas, down to her white cowgirl boots.

"We were just messing around in Austin," remembers Rodriguez. "It was 107 degrees that day, and we were drinking Tecate beers and hanging out at Roadhouse Relics. And I just loved the pictures so much that we used them. But this time around we did it in a studio and I got to spend two weeks talking about clothes and trying new things, so it was a totally different experience."

For the photo on the back of the CD, Rodriguez looks like an entirely different woman, in a strapless evening gown, black net stockings, heels, hair artfully teased, a judicious application of makeup. Sitting on a stylish white couch, more penthouse than roadhouse, with an electric tenor guitar (not a fiddle) beside her.

She Ain't Me, says this photo to anyone who arrives with preconceptions from Carrie's previous work. So, who is she? That was the scary part.

— Carrie Rodriguez

"I actually went through a lot of agony, a lot of turmoil and self-doubt that I had to sift through," she says of the album's birthing process. "The record label helped me a lot and was just so supportive. It was like, *Carrie, you've just got to try it. I know it's scary to try something without Chip, but I think you should do it. See what happens.* And I'm really glad I did. There were moments when I felt like giving up, when I wondered whether this was any good. I mean, Chip, he's so experienced, he's written a million songs, and when you're working with him, if he says, 'I think this is great,' it's easy to believe that. But take him out of the picture, and I have to kind of decide for myself."

Another crutch no longer as available to her was her violin virtuosity, the essential element of her musical identity since grade school. Though it had highlighted her solo debut, she plays sparingly on *She Ain't Me,* and when she does, the instrument is just another element in the mix. It isn't until the opening moments of the album's fourth cut, "Absence" (written with Mary Gauthier), that the violin presents itself like a calling card.

"There were some more fiddle-y type things that I showed [producer Malcolm Burn] that didn't make it to the album," she says. "His advice was, 'You know I love your fiddle playing and this is great for your live show, but I think it would be nice for you to show another side of yourself, and not necessarily use that because you have it.' And, I guess, act more like a songwriter.

"Working with Malcolm, his influence gave it more of a pop sensibility," she continues. "He's a keyboard player too, and he plays on most of the tunes, and I'd never really played with a keyboard player. We just got a pretty different sound. To me it's far less folky and twangy than anything I've done."

Burn, via e-mail, comments that "*we* (Carrie, Mike Bailey her A&R person, and I) wanted the record to be song-driven, but in a less folky/country way I believe. Carrie wrote or co-wrote almost all of the songs for starters, so it is a departure from her work with Chip Taylor in that sense. Also, I believe this record sounds much more open and sonically pleasing than her past

"Remember that behind that sweet smile and voice is a conservatorium trained,

work. That's just my ego talking! Apart from that, the whole experience was really warm."

While Burn applies the signature sonics that have highlighted his own productions (Chris Whitley, Charlie Sexton, et al.) as well as his many collaborations with Daniel Lanois, the songs and the singing are the real revelations here. The array of illustrious songwriting collaborators enhances rather than overwhelms Carrie's musical personality, as the songs took her in a different direction even before she entered the studio.

"The first thing I wrote with Gary [Louris, who wrote four cuts with Rodriguez and provides harmonies on two] scared me a little bit," she says. "Because it was so different. And it was coming out of me! I would come up with a melody and a groove, and then we'd sit down and try to figure out what should we make this about. But the sound was so much more poppy than anything I'd done.

"It was hard not to write with Chip at the beginning of the process, because that was all I'd done in terms of writing. That's where my comfort zone was. But I did want to push myself in that regard, to see what else was inside that hadn't come out yet. And I think writing with new people helped me do that."

There's a cosmic spirituality to "Infinite Night" (the opening number, written by Rodriguez and Louris), a socially conscious anger to "Mask Of Moses" (directed at rulers who hide behind religion), and a sense of redemption to "Grace." Yet the predominant mood is yearning, the sense of reflective separation that pervades "Absence."

"This last year I've dealt with being separated from my husband more than ever," explains Rodriguez. "He's been touring with this Spanish pop singer for basically a year and a half. And I've been out touring with my band. And it has been very trying on both of us. 'El Salvador' [driven by Burn's rollicking keyboard] is actually very autobiographical, but there's a lot of songs about separation. 'Absence' to me is a song about being alone and figuring out how to make it work."

To that end, perhaps the album's most intriguing cut is "The Big Mistake," a song of regret, a plea for forgiveness and a sensual moan all wrapped into one. "Actually, 'The Big Mistake' is a little bit of a warning song that I wrote to myself," she says. 'The Big Mistake' hasn't happened yet, and I don't plan on it ever happening, but to me it was a song where I put myself into the situation of ruining a beautiful relationship for a meaningless night."

As a classically trained violinist with one foot firmly in the pop arena, Rodriguez also retains dual citizenship as a native Texan who relocated with her husband to Brooklyn. When we spoke, she was back in Austin over the Fourth of July weekend, visiting her mother and taping an "Austin City Limits" performance. The differences between this home and her other home could hardly be more striking.

"There's not a lot of similarities," she says with a laugh. "Brooklyn's another world. I live in the third floor of a brownstone in a Polish neighborhood. I walk to five different stores to buy my groceries and live a very different lifestyle than I do down here. I love living in New York. I love being 15 minutes away from Manhattan and being able to see everything from a classical Indian concert to a singer-songwriter to a great jazz bill at the Village Vanguard. And I like being crammed in there with all those people. You walk out of your door and you're immediately entertained.

Magna Cum Laude graduated, world-class instrumentalist."   — *David Rodriguez*

"On the other hand, I'm sitting on the front porch of my mother's dome — she lives in a dome off of Bee Caves Road [in the rolling hills just west of the city] — looking at beautiful cedars and prickly pear cactus. And there's green all around me. And it feels really good. So I do miss this, I do."

Since her new album is as different from her previous work as Brooklyn is from Austin, it's tempting to claim that *She Ain't Me* represents the biggest artistic leap of Rodriguez's life. But the truth is that her life represents a series of such leaps — the leap from her Suzuki classical training to the folk clubs, the leap from Oberlin to Berklee, the leap to the Texas dancehalls and then to Chip Taylor's band, the leap to duet partner and then solo artist. Even if past is prologue, it might be hard to tell from *She Ain't Me* where Carrie is likely to land next.

Asked if he is surprised by the way his daughter's career has progressed, David Rodriguez replies (from his home in Holland, which is a big leap from Austin), "Yes and no. Yes, because I know how hard it is to get a break in this business. So, I'm grateful that she's progressed to this level. On the other hand, the girl has worked really hard. Remember that behind that sweet smile and voice is a conservatorium trained, Magna Cum Laude graduated, world-class instrumentalist. She could be the Pat Metheny of violin if she wanted that. Might still, who knows?"

Longtime ND *senior editor Don McLeese is amazed that he and his family have lived longer in Iowa than they did in Texas.*

NEW WOR

LD ORDER

A change in singers
and percussionists
broadens the big-tent
perspective of the Duhks

by **ROY KASTEN**
photographs by **LAURA CROSTA**

It's never long before genre breaks down. Music, the sound and experience of it, has more force than the forms behind it. Popular music is by definition a mixture of genres, a necessary combination of inherited structures and styles, but it's also about the instability of the conventions to begin with. If there ever were fixed forms such as bluegrass, bebop or punk, they didn't last in pure states for long. It's the conviction and skill with which great bands approach dynamic and fluid traditions that counts.

Winnipeg, Manitoba, string band the Duhks are to old-time music what Ozomatli is to rock, Weather Report is to jazz, Gnarls Barkley is to hip-hop. On their fourth album, *Fast Paced World*, released in August on Sugar Hill, the band doesn't just bend or break the conventions they know so well; they can make you forget the musical boundaries of genre exist at all. From the turbulent, quasi-gospel, quasi-rock opening track (and first single) "Mighty Storm" to the final, dreamlike, Latin-shaded ballad "I See You," and all the hybrid instrumentals and personal pop tunes between, the album makes an argument for another kind of world music, a utopia of sound, with tradition at the acoustic axis, and freedom spinning furiously around it.

The Duhks (and if anyone is still wondering, that's pronounced *ducks*) started as an idea in the head of Leonard Podolak, who had been leading the mostly Celtic and French-Canadian string band Scruj MacDuhk since 1995. Scruj focused largely on traditional tunes, familiar and obscure, combining guitar, bodhran, banjo, fiddle and percussion, and garnering a number of Juno award nominations while building a decent following on the Canadian folk circuit. In 2001, the band dissolved, and Podolak considered how to build on what Scruj couldn't quite do.

"My personal thought was to have a great band," he explains, "a band that could be a festival band, but could also play small bars, rock clubs or concert halls, be able to play dances, play a cross between old-time, Irish and French-Canadian music, and have a percussion player. When the band first started, we had Rodrigo Muñoz, who played on our first album, and it's not like I had any understanding about the differences between Latin or Afro-Cuban or African percussion. But he joined the band and I started to learn about Afro-Cuban music. I had an idea of the band when I started. But I really had no idea where it would go. It became an organic, living, breathing thing."

Podolak, 33, grew up in a folk-filled household. His father, Mitch Podolak, was one of the founders of the Winnipeg Folk Festival and owned a vast record collection. When Leonard was 6, Mitch introduced him to the clawhammer banjo. "It wasn't my thing," Leonard admits. "But I liked hearing my dad play." He moved to piano, played keyboards in a Guns N' Roses cover band, and then rediscovered the banjo when he heard Béla Fleck & the Flecktones in Winnipeg. He attended banjo camps in North Carolina as a teenager, and fell under the spell of traditional music culture. He attended French immersion school, began learning about the Quebecois culture, and discovered that French-Canadian music was related to Celtic music.

"And not only that," he says, "but that Celtic music and old-time music have a lot of cultural cross-references as well. You learn to play an instrument and discover that a melody is a

The Duhks, up against the wall in 2008 (l. to r.): Jordan McConnell, Tania Elizabeth, Christian Dugas, Sarah Dugas, Leonard Podolak.

The Duhks at Antone's during SXSW, 2005.

string of notes, and it doesn't matter where the tune comes from. You can play any tune on any instrument. I started to learn to play reels and jigs on the banjo. So Irish and old-time was my starting point, but then on our latest record, I'm playing a horn line, or I'm trying to imitate a slap bass, get funky. To anyone else it might just sound like a banjo!"

By January 2002, the Duhks' original lineup had come together: Podolak on banjo, Jordan McConnell on guitar, Tania Elizabeth on fiddle, Jessica Havey on lead vocals, and Rodrigo Muñoz on percussion. In 2003, the band's self-released debut *Your Daughters And Your Sons* established their spontaneous approach to old-time fusion: They merged a traditional fiddle tune with a Woody Guthrie composition, and covered Gillian Welch's "Rock Of Ages" with the same energy as they did little-known Toronto songwriter Kat Goldman's "Annabel." The title track, written by renowned Irish singer and songwriter Tommy Sands, announced the band's political idealism: "And though your body's bent and low/A victory you have won/For you sowed the seeds of justice/In your daughters and your sons."

"The vibe of the band has always been to play the music that we like and that we're good at," Podolak says. "And to learn from each other, share with each other. It's never been just one person's idea of what should be going on. We try to operate as a collective, all for one and one for all. Our band is like a rolling festival. If you wanted to describe the different styles, it would be like a big world festival."

The band's breakthrough in the U.S. came at the Suwannee Springfest in Live Oak, Florida, in 2003. Booked just three weeks before the event, they closed out the Friday-night concert. A Sugar Hill intern saw the band and took their self-titled debut back to the label, leading to their signing some 18 months later, and the re-release of the debut.

The band's self-titled 2005 album was produced by Podolak's hero Béla Fleck and Gary

The Duhks, 2005 lineup (l. to r.): Scott Senior, Jessica Havey, Leonard Podolak, Tania Elizabeth, and Jordan McConnell.

the next run of it." — Leonard Podolak

Paczosa (a veteran Nashville engineer and producer). The album pushed further into progressive string-band music and emphasized their newest member, percussionist Scott Senior (who had replaced Muñoz). They juxtaposed familiar traditional numbers such as "Wagoner's Lad" and "True Religion" with Leonard Cohen's "Everybody Knows," and connected Sting's anti-war hymn "Love Is The Seventh Wave" with fiddler Tania Elizabeth's composition "The Arch Of Abundant Love." They turned to songs written by contemporaries such as Ruth Ungar (of the Mammals) and approached them as vehicles for musical discovery, while still keeping the lyrical power of folk classics such as "Dance Hall Girls" (written by fellow Canadian Allan Fraser) in the mix. The band landed a half-hour spot on NPR's "All Things Considered" and won a Juno award for Best Roots and Traditional Album. The record sold over 40,000 copies, moving the Duhks to the forefront of a contemporary string-band scene that had its own momentum.

For all their individual talents, the Duhks' career owes much to the evolution of that musical culture, with its growing and changing audience, and to the burgeoning festival scene, which has played a pivotal role in popular music this decade. Merlefest, Telluride, Bonnaroo and Wakarusa, along with scores of smaller folk and roots festivals, have become more than just anchor dates for summer touring schedules. They've become subcultures unto themselves, and the Duhks have drawn energy and inspiration from them.

"The fact that there's now a generation of musicians of roughly the same age that comes together with a festival scene and circuit," Podolak acknowledges, "that's made it easy to make friends and have a community. And the different festivals have volunteers, and the volunteers have crews, which become social circles. Even if the festival only takes place for a few days, people think about it and get together every year to take part in this

The Duhks, 2008 (l. to r.): Leonard Podolak, Jordan McConnell, Christian Dugas, Sarah Dugas, and Tania Elizabeth.

thing. It becomes a bigger part of their lives. The whole festival business is really reliant on people who don't play music professionally. The community within the scene is a natural progression from the grass-roots aspects of the scene itself. And I think it has a lot to do with the people who inspired us. We're just the next run of it. It's sort of like pent-up energy in a way."

For their third album, 2006's *Migrations*, the Duhks turned to Tim O'Brien, who co-produced the album with Paczosa. They furthered their political idealism with a delicate version of Tracy Chapman's "Mountains O' Things" and added more gospel and blues influences, notably on Havey's growling delivery of "Ol' Cook Pot," "Heaven's My Home" and "Moses Don't Get Lost." They tested the contemporary possibilities of reels and jigs on original and traditional instrumentals, and com-

Sarah Dugas

bined uilleann pipes and bouzouki with Senior's arsenal of Latin and African percussion. The band garnered a Grammy nomination for Best Country Performance By a Duo or Group With Vocal for "Heaven's My Home."

But shortly after the awards ceremony (Alison Krauss & Union Station won, for "Restless"), Havey, the singer behind that performance, decided to leave the Duhks.

"It wasn't for her anymore," Podolak says, "the life on the road, the hectic schedule, driving for hours, months at a time. It's hard to say exactly. Bands evolve and change. It's really the best thing for everybody." Havey is now working with a neo-soul backing band called the Quirks and touring intermittently.

Percussionist Scott Senior also departed (wishing to spend more time with his family), and the Duhks moved quickly to find replacements. Podolak turned to Christian and Sarah Dugas, fellow Winnipeg residents Podolak had known for years. Christian was the percussionist in Scruj MacDuhk, and Sarah had guested on the Duhks' first album. When Podolak approached the siblings, they were part of an adventurous world music band called Madrigala, composed of seven singers who sang in sixteen different languages. The Dugases adapted, almost instantly.

"We all feel pretty settled in the lineup changes," Sarah says. "When I first joined I had to dive in, so the feeling of being new went away quickly. My brother also came in without having done any shows, and he just hopped right on."

As the Duhks' new lead singer, Dugas, who's 24, brings a warm, soul-based approach that recalls Havey's, but also widens the range, with a jazz and cabaret feel. Like the other Duhks, Sarah and Christian started early in music; they were swept into performing by their parents, who formed a family band when Sarah was 7 and Christian was 9.

"We started touring across Canada, doing folk festivals and folk shows," Sarah says. "We even played 'Sesame Street.' That's what started our professional careers. We would always belt out songs at the top of our lungs and harmonize around the house. And my brother started playing drums as early as he could hold a stick in his hands."

The reconstituted Duhks wasted little time in beginning the work that would result in *Fast Paced World*. This time they turned to the basement studio of rock and country guitarist and producer Jay Joyce (who has worked with Shelby Lynne, the Wallflowers and Patty Griffin), but without any fixed material or clear plan for the album.

"It was like, who wants to go first?" Podolak laughs. "Sarah brought some of her own material, but it was a month of discovery, of sharing and learning. It was very open. Most of the ideas we tried, some we didn't. I wanted to do a song by Big Country, 'Thirteen Valleys,' but Sarah didn't want to sing it. And that's as far as it went! And that was fine. You have to respect that.

It's still a great song, I'm still going to love it the rest of my life. But I'm not going to play it with the Duhks."

On *Fast Paced World*, the band again pulls from a wide variety of source material and inspirations, including their own families. The opening track, "Mighty Storm," is a traditional tune about the 1900 Galveston flood that was recommended by Podolak's father.

"He has been a cool source for material," Leonard says. "On our first record he suggested 'Leather Winged Bat.' On our second record he suggested 'True Religion.' Or maybe that was me! I don't know. But ['Mighty Storm'] is a perfect example of taking a traditional chestnut and reworking it. We got the version from Eric Von Schmidt, and it was much more bluesy, in a major-y kind of way. Jordan played some minor chords, which gave it a darker, more rock feel, and Sarah changed the melody. The band changed it, then in the actual production it got morphed some more.

Jordan McConnell

"It's relevant to now. I saw yesterday on the news, the Mississippi is flooding, 36 people died, and the president flew over to take a look. There was no real coordinated effort to help out these people. The song says that Galveston had a sea wall to keep the water down, but Galveston

Tania Elizabeth

didn't have one, but the people were demanding one. That's how the folk process works."

While *Fast Paced World* retains the feel of a live, acoustic band captured in mid-rocking conversation with each other, its sound is crafted and shaped, with subtle effects, sonic dislocations and rhythmic complexities. It's not quite the band's *Kiko*, but it's close. Especially notable are fiddler Tania Elizabeth's string parts, which move in and out of the mix like shadowy figures.

"It was very spontaneous in a way," Elizabeth says. "When we rehearsed the album, I couldn't double or triple the parts. But I knew there was a string section that lived inside of me that would come out."

Though the album begins with two forceful political statements, the record is really about re-establishing the Duhks' group identity, with its new singer and a driving percussionist who has his own way with the band's Latin influences. They've never captured a fuller or more original Brazilian sound than on "Magalenha," a reinterpretation of a Sergio Mendez rendition of a Carlinhos Brown song. The album's hardest-rocking number is an instrumental — or rather a fusion of three distinct instrumental tunes — called "New Rigged Ship."

"One of the tunes is 'Cumberland Gap,' which I learned from a banjo teacher," Podolak says. "Another comes from the *Old Time Banjo Project*, which is kind of like *Led Zeppelin II* for the old-time scene! But the song is just what happens when you get these five musicians together in a room. Christian is a wonderful percussion player, but in his heart he plays the drums. But his approach is very musical. It's not just bash-your-head-off."

The album is also grounded by the songs of Sarah Dugas, who has been writing since she was a teenager. "Toujours Vouloir," sung entirely in French (the title translates to "Always Wanting"), shows her striking melodic gifts. "I had the melody since I was 18," she says. "We had so little time to come up with material for the al-

Christian Dugas

bum, so I mentioned the song, and it just kind of worked. Never having created with the Duhks, I didn't know what would work out of my own compositions. We were all a little stressed that we had to create this album in a month and a half, but it took shape in a really great way. The [song's] translation is basically: I hope that one day love will reign and money will lose its meaning."

On "This Fall," Dugas spins a melodramatic, almost paranoid narrative that's saved by the ferocity of the arrangement. "I was living in my parents' basement, which is where I presently live," she says. "I wasn't even that lonely this past fall. It was just a thought that came into my head, seeing couples settled into relationships. When I first wrote it, I thought, oh god, it's a show tune. And I'm not one for musicals. When I started to think about it with a different approach, a Tom Waits-y heavy vibe, more of a cabaret style, it took another shape for me. That's when I could take it seriously. It's dramatic, so it has to have that kind of passion and energy."

While the Duhks are not a political band per se, they embrace the principal political spirit of their age: environmentalism. Their focus on sustainability has become as practical as it is idealistic. Over the last year, they've developed a project called "Green Duhks," which focuses their environmental consciousness into a news-based website (greenduhks.com) and an activist program that other touring bands can learn from.

"We've been trying to go green as much as possible," Elizabeth explains. "It became obvious in the first few months of touring just how unsustainable it is to be a band on the road. The amount of water bottles we go through that we just threw out, and the amount of gas we go through. It was mind-blowing. We tried to think of things we could do, but we kept running into brick walls. We didn't have the contacts or the resources or the finances to make it happen. A year and a couple of months ago, we started working with Greg Ching in Nederland, Colorado,

about transcendence."   — Tania Elizabeth

Leonard Podolak

who has been our sustainability coordinator."

The band now has a recycling program on their bus, looks for environmentally friendly sponsors, is working on solar panels to power laptops and iPods, coordinates with their fans on carpooling, and supports local groups who are working on sustainable, cooperative projects. *Fast Paced World* will be their first album produced with recycled paper and soy-based ink.

Still, the Duhks' social consciousness isn't about to overtake their music. More importantly, their urge to expand musically doesn't threaten the collective voice that results from their individual talents. For every genre, form and style they fuse and refuse, integrate and provoke, they seem to be discovering what the forms mean to them as a band, making music in the here and now.

"As much as this band is about diversity," Elizabeth gauges, "it's also about transcendence. Yes, we all have so many influences, but when we step onstage, we are creating something totally new and transcending those genres. We are just being ourselves. When you hear Leonard play clawhammer banjo, you're hearing Leonard. It's his personality and way of thinking coming through. And that could be said for everyone."

Longtime ND *contributing editor Roy Kasten considers himself too old for Wakarusa, but he couldn't imagine a summer without Twangfest or the Austin City Limits Festival.*

MmM

AN EXTENDED DISCOURSE
ON THE VALUE AND VIRTUES
OF BUBBLEGUM ROCK 'N'
ROLL, AND HANSON.

YES, THAT HANSON.

by DAVID CANTWELL

Pop!

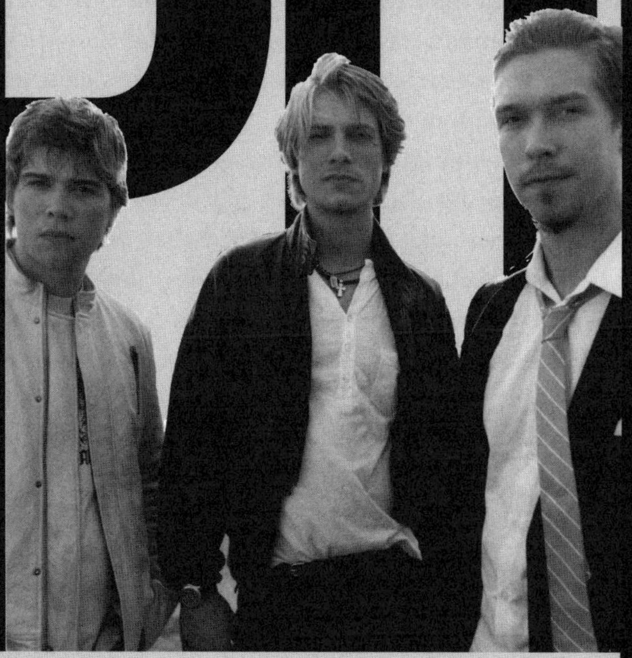

Hey, I know this band you should check out. What do they sound like? Well, this one song, "Great Divide," starts with this arresting jaggedy guitar part — like barbed wire electrified and hooked up to an amplifier. Then heavy, dramatic piano power chords start up. They have these great high, layered harmonies, too. Sounds really cool. Just one of the best rock 'n' roll bands working today. I'm telling you, you'd love them.

What else...they've worked in the studio with everyone from Beck-and-Beastie-Boys-collaborators the Dust Brothers to the Cars' Ric Ocasek to Danny Kortchmar. These guys have co-written with alt-popper Matthew Sweet, and with Brill Building legends Barry Mann and Cynthia Weil. They've performed onstage with Ben Folds a couple of times. I'll burn you a disc if you want. They're called Hanson.

Yes, that Hanson. I know, I know, the three kids who did "MMMBop." Wait, don't go! I'm serious here. Just give me a few minutes. Just hear me out.

But first, I have a question for you: What do you have against "MMMBop"?

Going on about "MMMBop" this far down the road is a bit like pestering "Billie Jean"-era Michael Jackson with questions about "I Want You Back," that first hit he'd made with his brothers when he was just 11, nearly fifteen years before. Within the Hanson saga, "MMBop" is a very long time ago as well. There have been four Hanson studio albums since 1997's *Middle Of Nowhere* and its lead single launched the brothers, if only momentarily, to heights of media overexposure few acts have scaled. And that's without counting the group's several live albums, collections of early recordings, and acoustic discs. It's been eleven years, and those cherubic boys are men now: Guitarist Isaac is 27, keyboardist and lead singer Taylor is 25, and drummer Zac is 22. All three are married, all three are fathers — Taylor has three kids, Isaac two — and they have worked hard to transform their fifteen minutes of fame into a real career. Still, most people know who they are only thanks to "MMMBop," and "MMMBop" is who they are. For Hanson, both for better and for worse, everything sooner or later comes back to that one damn song. People loved it. And then they loved to hate it.

"Actually, we got a lot of really good reviews at the beginning," Isaac Hanson tells me, recalling initial reaction to the album in the spring of 1997. He's right, too. You could fill a book with all of the favorable press the trio received out of the gate. "But then the record became omnipresent," he adds. "And that's when things changed." Incessant radio play, that ubiquitous MTV video, a best-selling "Official Book," innumerable *Teen Beat* covers, a "Got Milk" ad, several Grammy nominations, and 10 million albums sold worldwide — synced to a soundtrack of squealing, puppy-loving girls — will have a strong tendency to turn people against you. Particularly if you are a group of precocious, preposterously cute, and barely pubescent kids singing a tune so insanely catchy it can't possibly be ejected from the skull. A backlash was more or less inevitable, and, right on cue, "I Hate Hanson" sites dotted the internet. The New Radicals' minor 1999 hit "You Get What You Give" included the group in a list of "fakes" before rhyming "Beck and Hanson"

Pop stars Hanson (l. to r.): Zac, Taylor, and Isaac prove that the camera still likes them.
Photograph by Taylor Crothers.

"We weren't trying to appeal to a young audience. We wanted whatever

with "kick your ass in." On "Family Guy," the Hanson brothers were mistaken for "Children of the Corn" and shotgunned to death.

This was sometimes tough for the boys to take, even if they tried not to show it. "Some people make fun of Hanson," Isaac acknowledged to *Rolling Stone* in 1997, just as the tide was beginning to turn. "But you know what? I don't give a rip!" Mostly, the Hansons were good-natured about the backlash, even as it was slapping them in the face. That December, for instance, they parodied themselves on "Saturday Night Live." Will Ferrell trapped the brothers between floors on an elevator, then forced them to listen to "MMMBop" on a tape loop. The Hanson boys gamely bugged their eyes and covered their ears in mock agony.

So, yes. Hanson and "MMMBop" are forever stuck to one another like mac to cheese and Jan Brady to "Marcia, Marcia, Marcia." Like rock to roll. Backlash aside, this link has almost entirely been a good thing for the band, and will remain so as the brothers move forward. This is

most immediately true because "MMMBop" made them a pile of money — a windfall that allowed them to leave Island/Def Jam during the creation of their third album, *Underneath*, and to begin their own label in 2003. But the real value of "MMMBop," to Hanson as to the rest of us, is more basic: It is a great record. It is insanely catchy, of course, which for pop music is somewhere very near job one. And its buoyant beats and just-funky-enough scratching, courtesy of the Dust Brothers, launch the Hanson harmonies like colored balloons into a brilliant blue sky. Like "Walking The Floor Over You" in honky-tonk or "When A Man Loves a Woman" in country-soul, like grunge's "Smells Like Teen Spirit" or gangsta-rap's "Straight Outta Compton," Hanson's signature single is a perfect specimen of its type. And its type is bubblegum.

Well, that's not exactly right because bubblegum isn't exactly a musical type. You don't play bubblegum; you *are* bubblegum. The term is typically an adjective of derision — one aimed

Hanson (above) 1996, and (right) 2008.

at musical qualities which, if deployed by and for different groups of people, would be deemed not bubblegum at all but cool, hip, and good. This is why the power-pop of the Raspberries' "Go All The Way," say, or Matthew Sweet's "I've Been Waiting" and Nick Lowe's "Rollers Show" — or, for that matter, pretty much anything Paul McCartney has ever recorded, including his work with a little outfit called the Beatles — is almost never classified as bubblegum. It's why the Monkees' "Last Train To Clarksville," Rick Springfield's "Jessie's Girl," and the Bay City Rollers' "Saturday Night" almost always are. And it's why the proto-bubblegum of "Tutti Frutti," with its "A-wop-bop-a-loo-bop," has a credibility among those whose identity is bound up in such calculations that "MMMBop," with its "Ba-duba-dop-du-bop," is never granted.

Hairsplitting this fine is best explained by primarily extra-musical reasons: by the discomfiting juxtapositions of crass Saturday-morning-cartoon commercialism and safe-'n'-cuddly teen-idol sexual innocence with budding tweenage horniness; by the way bubblegum is not just

audience we could find."   — Zac Hanson

marketed to children but sometimes performed by them; by the assumption that while these musical treats may be tasty, they are nothing but empty calories; and by the hunch that there just has to be something fake going on here, after all. The music has almost nothing to do with it.

The Hansons learned these lessons the hard way. "I have been very frustrated of people's perception of me, thinking I'm a goody two shoes, this very innocent pop perception of me," Isaac admits. Then he adds: "But it's a misperception based on image, not on our music. I know who I am. We know who we are."

Who are they? Perhaps easier to pinpoint is who they are not. They are not a group, a la the Monkees, manufactured by television producers. The Hanson Brothers, as they were originally known, were singing their own songs, including "MMMBop," around Oklahoma and southern Kansas for years before Mercury signed them in 1996. They never had a Saturday-morning cartoon like the Archies or the Jackson 5, though on "Celebrity Death Match," the Hansons did

twice come to bloody claymation ruin at the hands of Marilyn Manson. And they never had a record on the back of a cereal box like the Osmonds or Bobby Sherman, though their likenesses did briefly appear on boxes of Eggo waffles.

Hanson will have to plead guilty to the offense of being kids when they started. Ditto the crime of having an audience full of the same, though as far as the brothers were concerned, this wasn't the plan so much as it was just how things played out. "We weren't trying to appeal to a young audience," Zac says. "We wanted whatever audience we could find." Young people latched onto the band in part, he figures, because it's "cool to be able to say, 'Hey, those kids are my age!'"

In what way band and audience were "innocent," sexually or otherwise, is tougher to say. Certainly, the sexual innocence of so-called bubblegum is exaggerated almost across the board. A bubblegum masterpiece like "I Think We're Alone Now," for example, is the antithesis of innocence, whether sung by Tiffany or Tommy James & the Shondells. Even a supposed trifle like Ohio Express' "Yummy, Yummy" conceals libido at its gooey center. There is only the one way to get love in your tummy.

Hanson's music and lyrics, even today, are notably lust lite. At the same time, their arrival in the Top 40 found them wise beyond their years. As the brothers will no doubt be reminding listeners for the rest of their days, "MMMBop" is a song about flickering devotion, about the transient quality of most relationships: "In an MMMBop they're gone." Or, as Zac frames it today, "Life is as quick and fleeting as this fake word we made up."

"Can you tell me who will still care...," the brothers ask in the song's lyrics. "You say you can. But you don't know." This was, and remains, fairly amazing, I think. At an age when most kids are earnestly proclaiming themselves Best Friends Forever, the Hansons were writing and singing about temporal impermanence and the inevitability of loss.

But so what? In pop, it don't mean squat if it don't got that bop. And "MMMBop" has *that* in surplus. High, sweet harmonies and nonsense syllables, a buoyant sing-along melody and, especially, the beat, the beat, the beat — these are sufficient ends in themselves, the record insists, desirable purely because they are pleasurable. It is these qualities that are bubblegum's chief virtues. Not coincidentally, they are also among the chief virtues of early rock 'n' roll, the selfsame virtues that have most often drawn each of us, in our succeeding generations, to enter the rock 'n' roll story. We tumble head over sneakers for one pure pop glory or another, for "All Shook Up" or "Big Girls Don't Cry" or "I Want To Hold Your Hand," for "Diddy Wah Diddy" or "Da Doo Ron Ron," for "MMMBop." And we fall for our record of choice primarily, perhaps even entirely, because we love its sound.

The sound is the key to the seduction, a formula that holds true even when our first love isn't a "silly" love song but a record that makes an important lyrical statement. I can brag to friends that the first record I ever bought was "War" by Edwin Starr. I'd like to boast further that this was because, at 8 years old, I was endorsing the song's insistence that war was good for "absolutely nothin'." But the truth is I bought "War" for one reason and one reason only: It sounded cool.

We love our bubblegum sounds with hearts wide open. Then the world sets to work. We are instructed in all sorts of ways, both explicit and implied, and by myriad sources — older siblings or best friends, college radio, rock critics — that our first love was harmless enough but not serious, not adult, and therefore slightly embarrassing. Our next step is predictable. We reject our object of devotion as just another youthful indiscretion. Loving the Partridge Family's "I Think I Love You" or the Hudson Brothers' "So You Are A Star" becomes, suddenly, the aesthetic equivalent of believing in Santa Claus. Henceforth, if we approach our bubblegum favorites at all, it is only with that face-saving, arms-length embrace known as Guilty Pleasure.

Ironic, that. For before it teaches us anything, rock 'n' roll shouts that guilt is pleasure's mortal enemy. "Feeling the music from head to toe," as Chuck Berry knew, is its own reward. Providing good vibrations — pulse-quickening and profound beyond words — is one of pop music's essential functions, and one that should take a back seat to no other. "MMMBop" pulses, like all perfect bubblegum, with deep-down wisdom that we forget at our peril: It ain't no sin to be glad all over.

The Hansons were born and mostly raised in Tulsa, Oklahoma, the sons of Walker Hanson, an oil company accountant, and his wife Diana. In the late 1980s, when the boys were approximately 9, 7 and 4, their father's job took the family out of the country. The brothers spent the next year or so discovering a new home and making new friends, then moving somewhere else to do the same thing, then moving yet again: Venezuela first, then Ecuador, then Trinidad and Tobago, and so on.

The boys had messed a bit with brotherly harmony even before they left Tulsa, but it was

we made up." — *Zac Hanson*

their year spent on the move when they got the bug, when "the spark for music," Zac says, "really showed up strong in our lives." They could harmonize and listen to music on their own, just the three of them, no matter where they were or when they might be headed somewhere else.

This was in 1988. Yet, in a twist that shaped the brothers profoundly, the music that fueled their musical spark was by then already 30 years old. Looking for music to occupy her children while they were in South America, Diana Hanson bought the boys an oldies cassette. Notably, she didn't foist her own music upon them — both Hanson parents are in their early 50s today and so, according to Zac, "grew up listening to Chicago, Three Dog Night, the Doobie Brothers, that kind of stuff." No, what their mom chose for them was a tape filled with tunes even she must have considered a bit quaint: the 1958 volume of Time-Life's *Rock 'n' Roll Era* series.

The Hansons have emphasized this quirk of their biography for more than a decade now, and it explains a great deal. "We just fell in love with that tape," Isaac recalls. "It had 'Johnny B. Goode,' 'Summertime Blues,' 'Splish-Splash,' 'Rockin' Robin,' and a lot of others. I was 9 years old when we got that tape, and I basically memorized it."

In addition to the tunes above — which, I discover later, Isaac has listed in order of their appearance, so he's not kidding about memorization — the Time-Life tape is packed with hits by a veritable Songwriters' Hall of Fame: Leiber & Stoller (the Coasters' "Yakety Yak"), Phil Spector (the Chantels' "To Know Him Is To Love Him"), Chuck Berry again ("Sweet Little Sixteen"), Huey "Piano" Smith ("You Just Don't Know"), Little Richard ("Good Golly Miss Molly"), and Otis Blackwell (Jerry Lee Lewis' "Breathless"), among other masters of the pop form. The boys couldn't stop listening and singing along, working out harmonies. When the Hanson family returned to Tulsa in 1989, the brothers quickly scooped up the remaining entries in the series, extending their love of old-time rock 'n' roll through the British Invasion and beyond.

"I think that fluke put us on a path that was very different from where we might have gone otherwise," Isaac says, referring to his mother's spur-of-the-moment cassette choice. "Because after that tape, we became obsessed with early rock 'n' roll. We couldn't have asked for a better education on what makes a great pop song."

If that's true, if Hanson learned more from those Time-Life tapes than they ever learned in school, what exactly were the lessons?

"We like songs," Zac says. "We like melodies. I like songs to have bridges. Most of those songs were three minutes or less, and it was all about what's the hook, what's the thing that's going to grab you and will make you want to play it four times in a row because you love the song so much.

"It wasn't the Flaming Lips version; there wasn't any *Dark Side Of The Moon* yet," he continues. "It was the origins of rock 'n' roll that we liked, and so we grew up wanting to find hooks. We're still that way. The songs we write are trying to find that musical part that will keep people humming the song in their heads."

The brothers' tutelage in melody and hook proceeded more formally during the recording of their first album, *Middle Of Nowhere*. "MMMBop" was theirs, but the boys co-wrote the album's second single (the Motown-on-steroids anthem "Where's The Love") with producer Mark Hudson, a former Hudson Brother and onetime teen idol himself. They collaborated with famed Mann-Weil songwriting team for the elegant ballad "I Will Come To You," their third single and second top-10 hit. "We were like, Wow," Zac gushes. "You wrote 'Who Put The Bomp In The Bomp-a-bomp'?"

Perhaps the most impressive cut on the album, though, is credited only to "I. Hanson/T. Hanson/Z. Hanson." A slow-building, gospel-inspired ballad, "With You In Your Dreams" is dedicated to the memory of the boys' grandmother and, a huge gesture, is written in her voice. The song is a dying plea, an urging of those left behind to keep on living. It springs from the mouths of babes, yet it is somehow a mature testament to the way those we love may continue to guide, influence and comfort (and haunt, as well, but that's a different song), even after they're dead and gone. Especially then. "And though my flesh is gone, I will still be with you," Taylor cries, and the corporeal nature of the language is striking, particularly if we are anticipating bubblegum innocence. When he continues, his words are as to-the-point, as artless, as real speech. "I don't want you to cry and weep/I want you to go on living your life." We hear in Taylor's agonized cries, and in his wordless moan, that this song in particular needs to matter. And, precisely because he is working from that point of view, it does.

We can see in retrospect that quite a few of the hits on the brothers' life-changing encounter with the Time-Life *Rock 'n' Roll Era* series are ur-bubblegum: Bobby Darin's "Splish Splash," for instance, or Bobby Day's "Rockin' Robin," which a barely teenage Michael Jackson would reprise to great success in 1972. Still other tracks on the tape — the Silhouettes' "Get A Job," the Monotones' "Book Of Love," and so much early rock 'n' roll, generally — possess a conspicuous sense of humor, a playfulness (both lyrically and in their rhythmic "sha-na-na" and "do-do-do" backing) that no doubt strikes some 21st-century listeners as verging on novelty. This lightness in approach invites some to hear the songs as great fun, and nothing else. But such reactions sell the songs and performers short. They miss the emotional dimensions beneath the sunny surfaces, the way that this fun is very serious fun indeed.

"Remember when rock 'n' roll was just fun?" It's been a long time now, but that's the question I remember being asked by one of those not-available-in-stores TV offers; perhaps it was even an ad for Time-Life's *Rock 'n' Roll Era*. At the time, the question annoyed me. Rock 'n' roll had never been just fun, I complained. Elvis and Fats and Chuck and Buddy, Little Richard and

education on what makes a great pop song."   — *Isaac Hanson*

James Brown and Ray Charles — these people changed the world. For the better.

I still believe that, but today I also take the ad's point. For one difference between the music of the *rock 'n' roll* era that inspired Hanson, albeit three decades after the fact, and the music of the just plain *rock* era that followed and then largely replaced it, is that the latter, particularly in its mainstream version, has become less and less willing to have fun. It has both acquired and lost dimension. After Dylan and the Beatles, pop musicians aspired to introspection and profundity, seriousness. This newfound depth, rather this new kind of depth, was freeing in countless amazing ways. Rock 'n' roll could be about anything that life was about. Yet it hasn't been. These new opportunities have been accompanied by new limitations, by the exclusion of emotions and approaches we still need because we are human: levity, goofy exuberance, sweetness, silly love songs, falsetto tenderness, and songs that say, "I could cry, but let's dance instead." The ironic result is that today's mainstream rock is typically far more segregated and often more one-dimensional than the seemingly simple, era-of-segregation music it replaced.

All of that to say just this: Hanson is not a rock band; they play rock 'n' roll. Their aim has remained true to that tradition straight along. On *Boomerang*, a pre-fame disc that the boys made to sell at county fairs and street festivals, they include a version of another Lieber & Stoller-penned Coasters hit, the still-hilarious "Poison Ivy." On *Live At Albertaine* from 1998, they kick things off with a medley of "Gimme Some Lovin'" and "Shake A Tail Feather" (late-'60s hits for, respectively, the Spencer Davis Group and James & Bobby Purify). Fittingly for youngsters so prematurely ambitious, they also include on that disc a cover of the old Barrett Strong hit "Money (That's What I Want)," a song covered so often over the years it must be considered on the short list for Rock 'n' Roll National Anthem.

"When we came back [to Oklahoma]," Zac explains, "we already loved those kind of songs so much that we didn't do what a normal kid might've done. We didn't turn on the rock station or the new pop station. We turned on the oldies station because that's where we could hear the songs we knew and other songs like that. It's not that we didn't like Nirvana and grunge and all that was happening then, we just didn't listen to it, we didn't know much about it. It was '50s and '60s music that we were in to, and '70s music too. The music of the '80s and '90s was mostly lost on us.

"I think this is why we don't sound quite like anyone else," he says. "I mean, not like any of our contemporaries."

Hanson has traveled a great distance since the stardom that followed *Middle Of Nowhere*. They quickly released both *Live At Albertaine* and *Snowed In*, the latter maybe the best pure rock 'n' roll Christmas album since they heyday of Phil Spector and James Brown. It wasn't until 2000, however, that they released a proper follow-up to their debut.

This Time Around contained a baker's dozen of hook-drenched, swollen-hearted Hanson songs, with no co-writes; the title track became the band's fourth top-20 hit. Like many Hanson songs, "This Time Around" is about refusing to "give in to the given," about pushing back when we're told that "dreams should stay in your head." This is an "important" message, though hardly a fresh one; it is, for instance, what every third country hit has proclaimed for several years now.

But Hanson's version of the theme still compels — first and mostly because of the music, which is its own reason for living, but also because the brothers never overlook, as so many writers do, the only reason the message matters. You must hang on to those who are most precious because…*you are going to lose them*. You should never say die because…*you are going to die*. More than a few Hanson songs come off akin to "The Death Of Ivan Ilyich," but with key changes and a good beat you can dance to.

It took four years for the release of Hanson's third studio album, *Underneath*. The delay is a tale of corporate tone-deafness and double-talk that is all too common in today's music industry but still would need to be seen to be believed. Fortunately, we can see it: *Strong Enough To Break*, a documentary film about the making of *Underneath*, has been presented on college campuses across the country and is also available on YouTube, in a thirteen-part series that ends with the boys, now all young men, acquiring their freedom and starting an indie label. (Episode 5, which captures the brothers receiving a cell-phone call from their nemesis, Island/Def Jam executive Jeff Fenster, is highly, albeit queasily, recommended.)

It is a testament to the brothers that despite several semi-coerced collaborations, with both producers and songwriters, they were eventually able to release such a fine album on their own label, 3CG (for Three Car Garage, the name of a 1998 disc which collected the recordings that got them signed to Mercury). *Underneath* is an exemplar of 21st-century rock 'n' pop: It has a huge, shimmering sound, and its songs are earnest, dramatic, and ridiculously, preposterously catchy, especially "Penny And Me," tailor-made for a summertime, windows-down road trip; "Lost Without Each Other," co-written with Greg Alexander, the New Radical who previously desired to kick their asses; and the delicate, sweet-and-sour title track, co-written with Matthew Sweet. "I have to say that was the most successful co-writing session I've ever had," Sweet tells the brothers in *Strong Enough To Break*.

Sweet's claim is not especially surprising. For both he and Alexander trade in sunny, '70s-inspired power-pop, a rock 'n' roll style that is close kin to bubblegum, and one that is precisely the ground upon which Hanson is making its stand.

"We've been laughing recently," Zac says, "because we've been covering…the Doobie Brothers' 'Long Train Coming.' We've been laughing because we grew up on '50s and '60s music but we've somehow turned out to be a '70s band. Or at least that's the closest thing I can figure out to what we are. We have that soul backbeat but with a white-guy soul vocalist and, like a lot of '70s bands were, we're really into harmonies."

Indeed. While harmonies, particularly of the three-part variety, have all but disappeared from current rock radio, the '60s and especially the '70s were decades when the biggest bands were instantly identifiable by their distinctive harmony blends: the Beatles and the Hollies, Steely Dan and Fleetwood Mac, the Eagles and CSNY. There are exceptions, of course, but not many.

"More akin to bands like…Three Dog Night, the Bee Gees," Isaac says, seconding the emotion. "I don't mean we sound like any of those bands. But, like them, we have multiple vocalists and place a big emphasis on harmony, we have keyboards up front, and there's a groove that lets you dance to it.

out to be a '70s band." — *Zac Hanson*

"Bands that showed up in the '70s grew up listening to 1950s rock 'n' roll but were also influenced by the harmonies and song structures of the 1960s. And that's exactly what happened to us. Whether or not we do it well enough is a whole other question, but that's where we come from musically, even though of course we actually come from the '80s and '90s."

Hanson's most recent album, 2007's *The Walk*, is perhaps not quite as strong as their debut, but it comes close. "Running Man," with its bouncing piano and the five gut-punches of power chord that end the chorus, and "Tearing It Down," with snaking synth lines that make it the funkiest record they've ever made — these are among the fiercest power-pop to come along in a very long time. Best of all is "Great Divide." After an opening of great crunchy power chords, the brothers address how they know they are viewed, who they understand themselves to be, and the chasm between. At the chorus, Taylor, Isaac, and Zac sing:

I find hope in what eyes don't see
I find hope in your hate for me
Have no fear, when waters rise
We can conquer the great divide.

These are good words, I think. But the guitar and harmonies soar.

Lately it seems we've seen more very young pop acts than ever — the Jonas Brothers and Hannah Montana and so on. Some people blame Hanson for this, or, the same thing in their minds, they blame "MMMBop." I ask Zac, who is still only 22 himself, if he thinks there's any truth to that. "I'll say this," he muses, then redirects my question: "I hope for those kids that, one, they come out of this with their heads on OK. And two, I hope that, if they're actual artists, they get to make the music they want to make, and that people really hear it."

So often in this world we discover only what we expect to find in the first place. What we expect to find is further confirmation of who we understand ourselves to be, another bit of self-flattering proof that there was nothing out there — nothing of consequence, anyway — to discover in the first place. We do this, all of us, in large part because we don't want to look foolish. But we are bound in the process to miss out on things we might otherwise love. We deny ourselves pleasure we deserve.

Take this challenge. I've mentioned or alluded to some few dozen records throughout this piece, by both Hanson and many other acts. Throw as many of those as you can onto a couple discs, or drag them all into one playlist in your iTunes. Sprinkle some Beach Boys, Badfinger, Babys and Big Star throughout. Begin the sequence with "MMMBop" and save the final spot for Hanson's "Great Divide." Do that, and reach your own conclusions.

At the very least, this playlist I'm describing will give you a fair, if only preliminary, accounting of that wondrous tradition we might call the rock 'n' roll/bubblegum/power-pop continuum. You can title the playlist "MMMPop."

David Cantwell is a longtime ND *senior editor. In 1997, he picked* Middle Of Nowhere *as album of the year.*

a continuing meditation on the pop narcotic
by Paul Cantin

Younger than that now

Jonas Brothers photo by Jake Chessum

A tornado recently blew through my town in the guise of teen titans the Jonas Brothers. The newspapers reported that 2,000 fans — some who lined up for three days — turned out to watch siblings Joe, 18, Nick, 15, and Kevin, 20, conduct not a full-on rock concert, but a mere Q&A session at a local TV outlet. Many thousands more were on hand for their show at the local outdoor bandshell. Scalpers were said to be commanding $500 a ticket, and the screams of adolescent glee and ardent pop-punk echoed across the city.

Perhaps these Jonas kids are building a musical legacy that will last the centuries. Or perhaps, as the business hones in on its ever younger target demographic, the brothers are the latest to surface in the churn of modern popular music, which has lately produced in its wake Miley Cyrus, Avril Lavigne, the Backstreet Boys, Britney, Christina, 'N Sync, etc. Paralleling this tilt toward youthful hitmakers is a surge in younger practitioners of Americana, some profiled in these pages.

This tributary of music history has produced controversy, too. Whole forests have been hewn into pulp and vast oceans of ink have been spilled for pundits to decry this perceived trend. The internet was seemingly invented for assessing via blog the suckiness of the latest moppet with a mike. Elton John (about 23 when he hit with "Your Song") moaned to the BBC that the current crop of young artists were like "packets of cereal." By which we take it Elton meant packets of really, really bad cereal.

There seem to be two narratives competing as an explanation for the phenomenon. The first let's call the *Logan's Run* theory, after the 1976 sci-fi movie cheesefest that envisioned a dystopia where citizens are permitted to live in splendor for 30 years, before being forced to make an abrupt and fatal exit (see also: Menudo). In this scenario, our culture increasingly lavishes rewards on the young, while denying those same attentions to the silverbacks. The second is the *Lord Of The Flies* theory, where the kids simply have taken over and anarchy reigns. Forget Hillary Clinton: Hillary Duff for President!

The perception of a generational insurgency is the product not simply of younger and younger kids clawing their way into the public consciousness or being rammed into our ears and eyes by a rapacious, youth-obsessed music biz, but at least partly because rock critics and culture commentators are, well, mostly old(er). The career duration of most music critics exceeds the popular reign of the vast majority of musicians, so writers who sneer at the latest crop of kids hitting the charts could be like a vintage sportswriter complaining that teams are drafting too many youngsters, and why can't they keep the older players? Granted, sport requires a certain degree of vigor not necessary for the performance of music, and if the rookies are inept when compared to the aging veterans, then those complaints are justified. But there is myopia in the ageism conveyed by some anti-pop commentaries. After all, when Buffalo Springfield made its first record, Neil Young was about one year older than the oldest member of the Jonas Brothers.

The superficial evidence suggests that, in music, being young doesn't hurt. Before we look down our noses at these junior phenoms, we would do well to consider at what age many of the most revered performers made an impact. Many of those pantheon artists made a mark when they were closer in age to Aly & AJ than they were to the culture critics who decry youthful barbarians at the pop-culture gate. The following assessment isn't scientific by any stretch, and there are examples of singers, songwriters and musicians who find their mark later in life, or reinvent and renew themselves throughout their career. But a highly selective look at the evidence suggests that if you haven't reached a creative apex by the age of 25, you might want to set aside the guitar and consider applying to college. (All ages are approximate, and declarations of significant work are subjective, of course.)

Elvis Presley was about 19 when he cut his epochal sides for Sun Records and 21 when he broke out with "Heartbreak Hotel." Gram Parsons was 22 in 1968 when both the International Submarine Band's *Safe At Home* and the Byrds' *Sweetheart Of The Rodeo* were released. As mentioned, Neil Young was 21 when Buffalo Springfield put out their debut album; he was 24 when Crosby, Stills, Nash & Young issued *Déja Vu*. Bob Dylan already had a successful career as a folk singer to risk when he went electric at 24. When The Band's *Music From Big Pink* came out, Robbie Robertson was 25. Van Morrison was 23 when he realized *Astral Weeks*. The Beach Boys' *Pet Sounds* was helmed by 24-year-old Brian Wilson.

Bill Monroe was 25 when he cut the first of some 60 sides for Bluebird. Hank Williams was about 24 when he recorded "Move It On Over"; he made "I Saw The Light" the following year and was, relatively speaking, an elder statesman of 28 when he hit with "Hey, Good Lookin'" and "Cold, Cold Heart."

And just to make sure we have our alt-country bases covered, Jay Farrar was 23 when Uncle Tupelo's *No Depression* came out; Jeff Tweedy was around 26 when *Anodyne* dropped. Interestingly, when Son Volt's *Trace* came out in 1995 and Wilco's *Being There* was released in 1996, both men were about to turn 30, and to this day those records are, to my ear, among the quintessential musical documents of that transitional time in life.

There doesn't appear to be a lot of literature discussing the relationship between age and creativity, although University of Chicago Professor of Economics David Galenson, author of *Painting Outside The Lines* and *Old Masters And Young Geniuses*, has proposed that there are two types of artists:

1. Conceptual artists who break with tradition and do their boldest and best work in their youth (think Orson Welles).

2. Experimental artists who fiddle within the confines of established modes of expression, may achieve some success throughout their career, and may peak late. (K.T. Oslin was in her mid-40s when she first hit with "'80s Ladies"; Grandma Moses was in her 70s when fame found her as a painter.)

Galenson's theory goes some way to explaining why Irving Berlin was 58 when he enjoyed a Broadway hit with *Annie Get Your Gun*, and how Paul McCartney co-wrote "A Day In The Life" at 25 but blessed us with *Memory Almost Full* at age 65. Still, Galenson's nomenclature is confusing. Berlin is, in Galenson's grid, an experimental artist, albeit in a very different sense than the way Karlheinz Stockhausen is considered an experimental musician. McCartney is, by the same token, a conceptualist, but *Wings At The Speed Of Sound* is not a concept album in the same way that, say, Styx's *Kilroy Was Here* might earn that label (or epithet).

We'll need to wait a few years in order to determine the enduring value of the Jonas Brothers' "Burnin' Up," but the theories don't really explain the crucial question: How do some young artists manage to create from their limited experience works of art that continue to strike chords — sometimes different chords in different ages — for generations?

The doomed British folk singer Nick Drake failed to secure much notoriety over the course of three albums, withdrew at 24, and was dead two years later at 26. When his music finally did find an audience in 2000 — via, of all things, a Volkswagen commercial — Drake would have been 52. It took a further 26 posthumous years for the world to catch up to Drake. What did he know then that we're just figuring out now?

On The Kinks' LP *The Kinks Are The Village Green Preservation Society*, there's a song called "Do You Remember Walter?" that describes a meeting between old friends which ends in disappointment:

Walter, you are just an echo of a world I knew so long ago

If you saw me now you wouldn't even know my name

I bet you're fat and married and you're always home in bed by half past eight

And if I talked about the old times you'd get bored and you'll have nothing more to say

Yes people often change, but memories of people can remain

For years, I had interpreted this to be Ray Davies' critique of people who lose their grip on their youthful zeal. But at 44, I realize things about the past and old friends and myself that Davies seems to have recognized when he wrote it. Now I hear the song as a sly reversal on the unreliable narrator, who can't let go of the past and cannot, like Walter, just get on with his life. Walter isn't a sellout; he's the hero of the song. Or so says fortysomething me.

But here's the twist: Davies was reportedly 22 when he was working on the *Village Green* songs, and 24 when the album was released. How could he possibly have understood, much less articulate so succinctly, a phenomenon that seemingly requires the passage of a certain number of years and experiences before it hits you? The truth is, both interpretations of the song are valid, and whether Davies intended to imbed that ambivalence in the song doesn't really matter, because he had the artistry and intuition to structure the song so that it transcended his own experience and continues to speak to the evolving human condition.

We can't say that experience necessarily yields wisdom. There are many seasoned songwriters who invest in their work puerility and pusillanimity instead of the worldly insights of the ages. And most kids, given license to make music, will bash out vaporous pop noise, not revelations in 4/4. Rare is the musician who exceeds and connects to something timeless and truthful. That's why we celebrate it when we recognize it, in both the young and the old.

As a contributing editor with ND, *Toronto resident Paul Cantin profiled Wilco, Beth Orton, Kathleen Edwards and others. He predates "Barney" and "Sesame Street" and was raised instead on the Monkees' Headquarters LP, which he still considers a masterpiece.*

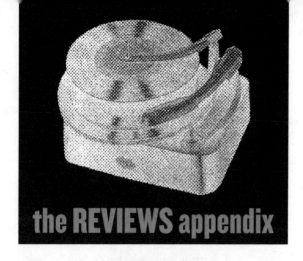

the REVIEWS appendix

EMPATHY LOVES COMPANY

MARK OLSON & GARY LOURIS

Ready For The Flood

(Hacktone)

by BILL FRISKICS-WARREN

THE JAYHAWKS were delivering on the promise of Gram Parsons' beloved, if slippery, notion of Cosmic American Music a good five years before anyone was calling it alt-country. Much like their fellow miniaturists the Silos, another band from the melodic interregnum between the noisy ascendancy of Jason & the Scorchers and Uncle Tupelo, the Jayhawks beguiled rather than bowled us over.

And not just sonically. Lyrically understated and unstinting in their generosity, both groups illuminated everyday struggles in ways that opened outward with disarming universality. Yet where the Silos ultimately proved a vehicle for the restless explorations of leader Walter Salas-Humara, the Jayhawks were essentially collaborative. Any measure of transcendence they achieved hinged on the intuitive give-and-take between principal song-writers Mark Olson and Gary Louris.

Early evidence of these bonds came with 1989's *Blue Earth*, a glorified demo session for Twin/Tone that shimmered with such splintered beauty as to render comparisons to Parsons and the Burritos irrelevant. Louris and Olson's alternately loamy and soaring harmonies were what got your attention, but their Bible-and-Woody-Guthrie-inspired populism struck as deep a chord. "Commonplace Streets" was how the title of one song put it, as epigrammatic a summation of the group's underdog-championing ethos as any.

Hollywood Town Hall, their 1993 debut for Def American, punched up the pastoral lyricism and little-guy solidarity of *Blue Earth* with major-label production. The group's real breakthrough, though — and, as it turned out, swan song — came two years later, with *Tomorrow The Green Grass*. The presence of Black Crowes producer George Drakoulias, string arranger Paul Buckmaster and pianist Karen Grotberg lent the album more of a pop sheen than its predecessors. Yet if anything, the added clarity only deepened the resonance of Louris and Olson's evocative originals.

Heartbreakingly tender, "Ann Jane" conjures images of abandoned children caring for one another as one of the older ones, beaming with pride, describes the meal of beans and Jell-O he's prepared for the song's namesake. In "See Him On The Street," a man wanders the town of his birth and, for undisclosed reasons, can't go home again. Failing, or perhaps refusing, to acknowledge his presence, his erstwhile neighbors act as if he's taken his own life. "If people call that suicide," mourns the narrator, "why'd I see him on the street today?"

Empathy, the ability to participate in the mystery of another — and, at best, to enter into another's suffering — ranks among the noblest of human emotions. It's also long been a hallmark of Louris and Olson's songwriting, a self-transcending impulse that remains at the forefront of *Ready For The Flood*, the duo's first album-length collaboration since they parted company, over artistic differences, after releasing *Tomorrow The Green Grass* in 1995.

Empathy brims from "The Rose Society," Louris and Olson's voices reaching to each other as if to bear one another up. "The look on your face when you start to remember," they harmonize, their notes breaking as they confront some unspoken sorrow. On "Bicycle," reassuring someone else, they sing, "It's hard to ride at night/On your bicycle, with no light to guide/Just take a chance and ride/…with no lights to guide." Crying steel guitar echoes their exhortation on the chorus.

Ready For The Flood is folkier and more intimate than anything Olson and Louris have done together; its austere arrangements — sometimes just a pair of acoustic guitars — underscore the emotional transparency of the duo's outpourings. "Are we going to find each other/In this great big dark of night," they ask in "Saturday Morning On Sunday Street." The gauzy interplay of their voices here is more Simon & Garfunkel (via the Everlys) than anything resembling roots-rock. In "Kick The Wood," buttressed by a weary backbeat, they sing, "Respect your own heart/Don't let it fall apart." Mining a similar folk-rock vein is "Life's Warm Sheets," replete with hushed harmonica and filigrees of fingerpicked guitar. "Life's warm sheets/They get turned down/You work and work/Then turn around," they sigh, conveying not so much warmth as a chilling awareness of their finitude.

A couple tracks on the record, notably the

ILLUSTRATION BY JESSE MARINOFF REYES

bluesy "Chamberlain SD," rock out a little, but on balance, the tempos and mood here are subdued, and sublimely so. In "My Gospel Song For You," backed by acoustic guitar and keyboards, they yearn, "I hold you inside/It don't matter, no matter the cost/I came back when you said/You needed me so bad." Later, amid the dappled Appalachian hues of "When The Wind Comes Up," they wonder, "Away, as I carry you inside this burning fire/Will you be there?/There's no home without you here."

"Bloody Hands," a bluegrass-inflected tale of murder and revenge that confronts evil in microcosm, seems to call all of this empathy into question. "What the mind forgets, the soul retains/All my love's in vain," Louris and Olson lament on the chorus. They may claim that their flood of compassion is of no account, but their great efforts to inhabit the struggle of the song's wronged mother and daughter suggest otherwise. The fact that the two of them care at all, that they have such fellow feeling for others who suffer, is enough to prove that caring matters. Empathy alone is never enough, not in the face of evil. But if nothing else, its expression, as Louris and Olson so exquisitely remind us, testifies to the possibility of participating in another's suffering — if only, however fleetingly, to redeem it.

RODNEY CROWELL
Sex & Gasoline
(Yep Roc)

HAS AN ARTIST ever enjoyed being unshackled from expectations more than Rodney Crowell? It has been more than a decade since he left his hitmaking days in Nashville behind — and/or since they left him. After his prolific run for Columbia Records ended not in a blaze of glory but amid the foul smoke of declining sales, compromised standards and hard self-criticism, he took time to ponder his role an artist, to question his methods, and to plot his return. When he resurfaced, his conviction recharged and his ambition newly lit, he staged a second act that would impress F. Scott Fitzgerald.

Mixing autobiography and fiction on *The Houston Kid* (2001), Crowell reflected on the pain and barefoot glory of his boyhood — one darkened by the beatings his mother took from his alcoholic father, among other crimes, and transformed by Johnny Cash's "I Walk The Line." On *Fate's Right Hand* (2003), he stared into middle age to confront his shortcomings and count his blessings, doing both so openly that you could almost feel his personal growth rubbing off on you. On *The Outsider* (2005), it was time for Crowell to go outward, via blistering, satiric commentaries on greed, hypocrisy, and the war-making politicians who "don't give one whit about the man on the street with his back to the wall."

To embrace these recordings was not to deny the indelibility of early Crowell classics such as "I Ain't Living Long Like This" and "Til I Gain Control Again," or the appeal of the pop-infused songcraft with which he and his then-wife Rosanne Cash ruled the new country roost in the 1980s. It was to recognize how powerfully the added layers of experience had served his unquenchable poet's desire to squeeze meaning from life — and to keep up with it, to try to help change it for the better.

Now comes *Sex & Gasoline*, and Crowell is stretching yet again. As you might guess from the title, he's not finished railing at slick politicians, sleaze merchants, and fresher signs of our declining civilization. This will give pause to critics who have detected self-righteousness in his rants, though it's hard to imagine anyone holding that against him when he takes aim at this culture's sexualization and commodification of young girls.

But working with producer Joe Henry, ambient rocker par excellence, Crowell mostly turns down his emotional thermostat to draw us into nuanced narratives that reflect his concerns — his states of being — as a husband, a lover, a father of daughters, a feminist. None of the songs have the buoyant melodic lift of "Earthbound" (from *Fate's Right Hand*) or the punch and groove of the title track to *The Outsider*. Which isn't to say there aren't some striking, and surprising, hooks. And there may be more going on under the surface — musically as well as thematically, thanks to bassist David Piltch's suggestive strokes and drummer Jay Bellerose's artful textures — than on anything Crowell has done before.

There's no lack of immediacy on *Sex & Gasoline*, a smart, live-in-the-studio production that puts Crowell's vocals up-front and without cushion while capturing surrounding details with vibrant clarity. "Who Do You Trust," featuring guitarist Doyle Bramhall III, catches Crowell in carousing blues-rock mode. But the album is more defined by songs such as "I've Done Everything I Can," a one-of-a-kind duet on which Crowell and Henry ruminate affectingly on fatherhood, on the agony of letting go. It's not often that two artists with their blend of passion and intellect share this kind of spotlight.

"Closer To Heaven," a kind of sequel to "Earthbound" in cataloguing things that make life worth living (as a bonus, Crowell lists things he has no use for, including sushi and golf), is an uplifting closing statement. Backed by gospel-style voices, he tells us he has no wish to be famous, "only to be happy wherever I am." If anyone has a third act in him, judging by the place he is now, it's Crowell. While so many artists of his generation are on the ground and heading for home, he's still years away from learning how to land.　— LLOYD SACHS

EMMYLOU HARRIS
All I Intended To Be
(Nonesuch)

IN 1995, Emmylou Harris took what seemed an incomprehensible left turn. *Wrecking Ball*, produced by Daniel Lanois, was an apt title for the album Harris made that year. On paper it was an odd match — a producer steeped in sonic modernity, best-known for the electronic ambience of his work with U2 and Peter Gabriel, paired with a singer who has always worn her rustic identity proudly, ever since she first emerged as Gram Parsons' duet partner in the early 1970s.

Improbably, however, that left turn proved to be exactly the right direction. Lanois' spooky ambience was the perfect aural complement to Harris' earth-angel mournfulness, and launching that voice into the stratosphere unlocked new universes of potential for her. What seemed like a bold (and possibly misguided) attempt at reinvention turned out to be a sharpening of focus.

Wrecking Ball has worn surprisingly well over the years, in part because Harris has developed Lanois' sound into something of her own. She kept to a similar course with two albums produced by Lanois associate Malcolm Burn, 2000's *Red Dirt Girl* and 2003's *Stumble Into Grace*, shaping a once-startling combination into a well-fitting sonic framework. Even returning to Brian Ahern — Harris' ex-husband, and producer of her first eleven albums — has not significantly altered the results. *All I Intended To Be* is her first full-length collaboration with Ahern since 1983 (and also her highest-charting album since 1981's *Evangeline*), yet except for a shade more prominence to acoustic instruments, its sound could just as easily have been fashioned with Burn or Lanois behind the board.

Harris is one of the most universally beloved figures in the music industry, and *All I Intended To Be* finds plenty of old friends dropping by to lend a hand. Dolly Parton, the McGarrigle Sisters, Vince Gill, John Starling from the Seldom Scene, and *No Depression* Artist of the Decade Buddy Miller all show up in key support roles, though there's no wresting the focus from Harris herself. You could put her in the bottom of a well, up against the Mormon Tabernacle Choir, and Harris' emotional quaver is still the first thing you'd notice. To say she's never sounded better is simply to note that she never sounds less than fabulous.

Harris wrote or co-wrote five of the album's thirteen songs, but the track list is as steeped in camaraderie as the credits. The very first track, John Wesley Routh's "Shores Of White Sand," is a song Harris has had her eye on ever since Ahern produced Karen Brooks' first version back in 1982 — and in fact, Harris uses Brooks' original backing track, featuring the late Keith Knudsen on drums. Mark Germino's "Broken Man's Lament" is another song Harris has had stashed away since it originally appeared 22 years ago, and it's a prime example of her versatility. Harris sings in first-person as a heartbroken working-class guy who drove his wife away; it's a bit of play-acting that should've been tough to pull off, but darned if she doesn't make you believe every word.

Songs by Tracy Chapman ("All That You Have Is Your Soul"), Patty Griffin ("Moon Song") and Merle Haggard ("Kern River") also get the Harris treatment, while Billy Joe Shaver's stately "Old Five And Dimers Like Me" provides the album's title phrase. "An old five and dimer is all I intended to be," Harris intones with duet partner Starling, the two sounding very much like the dear old friends they are.

If there's a flaw with *All I Intended To Be*, it's the album's uniformity of tone. Song after song plumbs mournful depths of sadness and longing; those who aren't already among the previously converted might find so much unrelenting melancholia a bit much to take. But that's who she is — and all she intended to be. — DAVID MENCONI

GLEN CAMPBELL
Meet Glen Campbell
(Capitol)

"THE REAL father of *ND* music is Glen Campbell," a rather influential music-industry figure contended in a note to me some eleven years ago. While I wouldn't quite concur with his assessment, he went on to make a reasonably compelling argument, grounded ultimately in his closing observation: "He's the guy that brought me, and millions, to country music."

Thing is, of course, Campbell has never really been country, or certainly never strictly so. Even his biggest country smashes — from the early Jimmy Webb classics "Wichita Lineman" and "By The Time I Get To Phoenix," to the career-zenith signature-song "Rhinestone Cowboy," to the Allen Toussaint-penned "Southern Nights" — took over the pop charts too, in much the same way that similar '70s artists such as John Denver and Olivia Newton-John crossed over. Perhaps the most revealing of his hits was a comparatively lesser-known tune, 1975's "Country Boy (You Got Your Feet In L.A.)," in which the title character laments being removed from his southern roots: "But your mind's on Tennessee." Never mind that Campbell was actually from Arkansas; the spirit was the same, and it seemed appropriate that he eventually returned to the region in his twilight years as a fixture in Branson, Missouri.

But it's precisely Campbell's long crossover career which makes *Meet Glen Campbell* not all that surprising, despite the initial shock-value of its track list: songs by Travis, Tom Petty & the Heartbreakers, Foo Fighters, Jackson Browne, the Replacements, U2, the Velvet Underground, Green Day, and John Lennon.

Campbell is, after all, an interpreter, and several of these selections aren't really all that much of a stretch for him, particularly because he and producer Julian Raymond were careful about which songs they chose from those artists' catalogues. "Femme Fatale" or "Foggy Notion," probably not; but the more obscure Velvets track "Jesus" speaks to Campbell's gospel leanings just fine. "Kids Don't Follow" or "Androgynous," no, but the latter-day Replacements ballad "Sadly Beautiful" proves well-suited to Campbell's voice and sensibility, all dressed up in strings and the backing vocals of Campbell's children. Early Green Day power-punk like "Longview" would be out, but their ubiquitous pop pleasantry "Good Riddance (Time Of Your Life)" is a gimme for Glen.

Some artists weren't even that much of a stretch. Jackson Browne's "These Days" was an easy choice — probably too easy, as it's by far the most-covered song in Browne's cata-logue. While Campbell's reading is pleasant and pretty enough, it might have been more revealing and magical for him to take on, say, "For A Dancer" or "Colors Of The Sun." Petty turns out to be the most natural fit, so much so that Campbell covers two of his songs, "Walls" and "Angel Dream" (both from the 1996 soundtrack album *She's The One*). John Lennon's "Grow Old With Me" works surprisingly well; like "Jesus," it appeals to Campbell's spiritual side, with its chorus chant, "God bless our love." One could argue that it's misrepresentative to cover Lou Reed and John Lennon and pick religious songs from both; but ultimately, the song matters more than the source, and Campbell's renditions come across as honest interpretations, even if his perspective may be different than that of the songs' authors.

Most successful, somewhat surprisingly, are the songs by the Foo Fighters and British band Travis. The latter's "Sing" leads off the record and features Campbell's strongest vocal performance, as he reaches for those emotional high notes like he did in his younger days. Dave Grohl's "Times Like These" is notable largely for its opening baritone-guitar and string-section riff, which immediately calls to mind "Galveston." Most unnecessary of the disc's eleven tracks is U2's "All I Want Is You"; there's little point in trying to compete with Bono's original vocal, and neither Campbell nor his producer bring anything new to the table.

What *Meet Glen Campbell* is *not*, to be certain, is a late-career resurrection a la Johnny Cash's *American Recordings*; nothing here is so revelatory in its melding of singer and material. Still, it's easily the most interesting record Campbell has released in years, a welcome reminder of his intrinsic appeal as a pop vocalist. — PETER BLACKSTOCK

MUDCRUTCH

self-titled

(Reprise)

TOM PETTY HAS always known the importance of being in a band, and Tom Petty & the Heartbreakers have been one of America's very best rock bands since their 1976 debut, with hits such as "Breakdown" and "American Girl" becoming the first of many. Petty and company were steeped in garage rock, British Invasion, southern rock and soul. They also played a more classic (and commercial) style of rock than the punk and new-wave groups of their day. In the 1980s they toured with Bob Dylan, sharing the bill and playing backup (Tom and Bob would later collaborate as members of the Traveling Wilburys). Petty also enjoyed solo hits such as "Free Falling," which fit right into a Heartbreakers concert. Thirty-two years and 50 million records down the road, Petty & the Heartbreakers played halftime at the Super Bowl and sat for a four-hour documentary directed by Peter Bogdanovich, *Runnin' Down A Dream*.

The early scenes of that documentary are a counterculture flashback, with Petty and his essential Heartbreakers — guitarist Mike Campbell and keyboardist Benmont Tench, both masters of their instruments — finding regional success in a hippie band with a world-class bad name, Mudcrutch. They were the hottest band in Gainesville, Florida, playing five sets a night at clubs such as Dub's, and promoting three successively wilder Mudcrutch Farm Festivals at the secluded farmhouse shared by Campbell and drummer Randall Marsh (the third festival got them evicted). Petty brought the band to California for a shot at the big time, but the first single

flopped, and they broke up. Petty may belong in a band, but he's also a ringmaster, so he moved from bass to guitar and formed the Heartbreakers with Campbell and Tench.

One strange long trip later, Petty called Marsh and guitarist-singer Tom Leadon (brother of Bernie Leadon, who played with both the Flying Burrito Brothers and the Eagles) to make the Mudcrutch album that never happened. Both had stayed in music; Leadon taught in public schools, while Marsh instructed private students. They gathered at Petty's place in Malibu, and things clicked again. Cut live in the Heartbreakers' rehearsal space over ten days, Mudcrutch is the best early-'70s country-rock album of 2008.

Mudcrutch is Petty's Rosebud because these guys were there when he became a band-leader. Petty reportedly wrote some of the new songs the night before they were recorded, and a few are better than others, but none stink, and all feature bandmates who are clearly looking each other in the eye and having fun. Compared to the Heartbreakers, Mudcrutch is closer to country than rock; they favor an organic, jammy sound to the Heartbreakers' more sculpted arrangements. Petty's back on the bass, and he's high in the mix, and while Campbell can't help but be the guitar star, he also shares leads with Leadon, who harmonizes with Petty and sings his own "Queen Of The Go-Go Girls." Tench plays fabulous keyboards throughout and contributes a snappy song called "This Is A Good Street."

Petty sings most of the rest. His best tunes include "Scare Easy," a pop-rock shuffler that would have fit comfortably on any of his recent albums, and a wickedly fun boogie, "Bootleg Flyer," a Campbell co-write that features twin-guitar passages straight from the southern-rock playbook. Cover songs delivered with exceeding confidence include "Six Days On The Road" and a Byrds chestnut from the Clarence White-era, "Lover Of The Bayou." The capper is Petty's "Crystal River," which takes the magic mushrooms with a gently psychedelic, near-ten-minute jam that suggests the Byrds meeting the Grateful Dead. The early-'70s rarely sounded this good.

The coastal Florida town of Crystal River is a short hop from Gainseville. Good times, man. Petty convinced the members of Mudcrutch to quit college and go to Los Angeles and become rock stars. Things didn't work out exactly as planned. But as everybody knows, there's always something special about your first love, your first band. For Tom Petty, who went to school on rock 'n' roll, Mudcrutch is the college reunion he'll never have.

— JOHN MILWARD

JOHN MELLENCAMP
Life Death Love And Freedom
(Hear)

SINCE I SEE no reason to reopen a debate with my esteemed editor, let's agree from the outset that there are no Chevy commercials here. The all-American title may be typical of the all-American artist, promising the sort of anthems that were once hit singles and later became advertising jingles. But the dominant verity throughout this song cycle is death, and death needs no advertisement. We're all gonna buy it, want it or not. And death typically isn't the stuff of hit singles, unless it happens to someone else, in a romantically tragic manner ("Last Kiss," "Teen Angel").

Unlike so many artists of his generation, Mellencamp is not only acting his age here,

he's sounding a decade or two older. In the unvarnished production by T Bone Burnett, you can hear every one of those cigarettes the Hoosier bard has smoked since the 1994 heart attack that almost killed him, in songs that sound more like a last will and testament than the life force that has long provided the muscle for even Mellencamp's darker material.

And much of it has been pretty dark, back to a little ditty called "Jack And Diane," where the sing-along chorus of "Oh yeah, life goes on," resolves itself as "long after the thrill of living is gone." Or the fist-pumping rebellion of "Authority Song," where "I fight authority" but "authority always wins." And whatever "Pink Houses" means, reducing the American dream to "little pink houses for you and me" isn't exactly manifest destiny.

But none of Mellencamp's music has been as bleak as this — as deathly as Bob Dylan's *Time Out Of Mind*, as stark as Bruce Springsteen's *Nebraska*, as infused with mortality as Johnny Cash's final recordings. So uncompromisingly, unflinchingly dark that you could hear the late Howlin' Wolf backed by the switchblade guitar of Hubert Sumlin on tracks such as "If I Die Sudden" and "Don't Need This Body." "I'm not afraid of dying, this life's been good to me," rasps Mellencamp on the former. "I got a whole bunch more than I deserve, now I will be free."

As for the latter, when Mellencamp proclaims "This getting older ain't for cowards" and describes himself as "washed up and worn out for sure," he leaves no reason to doubt him. Has anyone this side of Samuel Beckett written more of a staring-into-the-abyss admission than "Ain't gonna need this body much longer"?

The enlistment of Burnett marks the first time that Mellencamp has entrusted his music to a sole outside producer (rather than sharing credit as a co-producer) since he employed Steve Cropper in 1980 for *Nothing Matters And What If It Did* (another cheery title) as he attempted to bury his Johnny Cougar persona for good. Though Burnett has shown a Midas touch for transforming rootsy Americana into gold and platinum — from Counting Crows' *August And Everything After* to *O Brother, Where Art Thou?* and the recent Alison Krauss/Robert Plant collaboration — he has demonstrated throughout his career (and particularly on his solo albums) that making hits is less of a priority than serving the song, which he does here through judicious instrumental punctuation and his own electric guitar.

It's telling that Mellencamp voices the album's bleakest nihilism in a character song, as he snarls in "John Cockers" that "I used to have some values, now they just make me laugh." Yet the album's darkness eventually sees light, with "Mean" serving as a response to so much that has come before: "I'm not following your frame of mind/Complaining about this life all the time," he sings with uncommon tenderness. "Surely something good here as the world spins by/Could you please stop being so mean."

Is he singing this to John Cockers? Or to John Mellencamp?

As the celebration of his 1985 *Scarecrow* hit "Small Town" has decayed into the seediness of this album's "County Fair," *Life Death Love And Freedom* is Mellencamp's first for the Starbucks offshoot label Hear Music, the perfect musical accompaniment for a grande latte with an extra shot of cyanide. Yet ultimately it's an album about how death defines life, in this case a life lived with passion, courage and heart. He could rest his career on this.

— DON MCLEESE

AL GREEN
Lay It Down
(Blue Note)

FOR WANT, Al Green sings: First for want of a woman ("Tired Of Being Alone"), then for want of God ("Take Me To The River," and all the gospel albums that soon followed), and now…now, having presumably found and nestled himself safely these many years in the loving arms of both a good woman and his good God…now for the want of what?

A number of uncharitable answers to that question present themselves, but guessing at an artist's motivations is usually a fool's errand. (And unknowable, mostly, even to the artist.) The wanting, nevertheless, is an issue for Rev. Green because it is what has filled his voice, his songs, his pockets. And because it is what seems most missing from *Lay It Down*, the fourth album made during this second secular pass (not counting a Christmas offering).

Al Green returned to pop music in 1995, after an eighteen-year hiatus preaching and singing the gospel, with *Your Heart's In Good Hands*, produced by Arthur Baker, Narada Michael Walton, and Fine Young Cannibals David Steele and Andy Cox. (Pop music had, of course, changed some.) Two albums followed, reuniting Green with Willie Mitchell, with whom he cut his original hits, the ones we still hear on the radio. *Lay It Down* pairs Green with contemporary producers Ahmir "?uestlove" Thompson, of the Roots, and James Poyser, a keyboard player and producer with a long list of contemporary soul credits.

In their hands, Green wants for nothing. He is surrounded by the Dap-Kings Horns, the late "Spanky" Alford on guitar, and plenty of strings and voices; he duets with Anthony

Hamilton and Corinne Bailey Rae and John Legend; and they recorded it all in analog. He wants for nothing, except for songs, captivating hooks, phrases that return unbidden on long drives. *That*, he wants for. He wants for something to turn that voice loose on. He wants for something to want.

The opening duet with Hamilton, "Lay It Down," might be forgiven as a necessary excess — *all* those strings, touches of skating-rink organ, that huge chorus — if the melody line (or the words, even) weren't so lugubrious. So predictable. So uninteresting a set of lines to sing over and again, no matter how Green tries to stretch his voice around it.

Much of *Lay It Down* is like that. The other Hamilton duet, "You've Got The Love I Need," *almost* rouses itself toward ecstasy, but trails off into an Earl Klug-kinda guitar piddling. It is followed by the brutally banal "No One Like You" (and this is not to hold soul lyrics to, say, Dylanesque standards of profundity).

And then, after one has about given up, signs of life emerge. "Too Much," buried seven tracks in, has a beautiful, keening swing to it, and for the first time Green's voice soars and pleads and means it, man. Really means it. Is finally in the grip of that thing bigger than himself that he somehow taps into, whatever the thing that puts that joyous grin on his face during every photo session. (If you listen carefully toward the end of the song, somebody else on the session chimes in with an approving "whoa!" Amen to that.)

But even this moment of joy is undercut by the dull affair titled "Stay With Me (By The Sea)," the John Legend duet, everybody striving mightily for beautiful, lush sounds, but the song not quite opening up into anything that rewards their effort.

If nothing else worked, you could pass the album off as an honorable but unwise attempt to modernize Green's sound, as an effort by the producers to find their voice(s) around Green's.

Then one comes upon "All I Need" (again, buried toward the end of the album), which employs all the gadgets — horns, strings, a swelling chorus — and a glorious chorus cascading down Green's register. And "I'm Wild About You," which actually has a genteel (almost disco) funk to it. The concluding "Standing In The Rain" marches quite vigorously, too, Green's voice roughened up, the chorus behind him singing with more joy and less precision than throughout.

What Green wants, it seems, is another chance. A better chance.   — GRANT ALDEN

IRMA THOMAS
Simply Grand
(Rounder)

AT THE PotLuck Audio Conference this past June, famed New Orleans producer Cosimo Matassa leaned forward to make sure his audience understood. "Irma Thomas is more than a singer," he said. "She's an *entertainer*." The audience of young engineers, producers and recorders looked at him like he'd had a senior moment. "Entertainer" is the term reserved for the Vegas act — someone who does whatever necessary to please a crowd. Matassa used the example of Sammy Davis Jr., which didn't help. "Artist" seemed like higher, more appropriate praise; when Matassa explained that Thomas could make an audience feel something, that she could communicate emotions, the mood lightened a little, but people weren't really buying it.

Thomas' new *Simply Grand* has elements

of the entertainer, just as she does. Live, she gives the audience what it wants — usually her hits, regardless of the number of great songs in her catalogue — and her default vocal mode conveys a warm wistfulness when she thinks back on lessons learned the hard way. It's a crowd-pleasing, Oprah-esque voice, and when it's paired with the randiness of "(You Can Have My Husband But) Don't Mess With My Man," it's a winning combination.

For me, that voice started to ring a little hollow by the late 1990s. It's tempting to attribute Irma's rejuvenation to Hurricane Katrina, after which she cut "Backwater Blues" for the *Our New Orleans* compilation and recorded her Grammy-winning *After The Rain*, both of which established her as a remarkably nuanced blues singer. But check out "The Same Love That Made Me Laugh" on 2005's *I Believe To My Soul*, produced by Joe Henry. He cleared the deck of all extraneous instruments, all the familiar R&B horns, all the bigness, and made her the unchallenged focus. She responded beautifully, not simply expressing the emotion, but conveying the pleasure she took in using her voice that way. That rich musical experience provided the blueprint for producers Mark Bingham and Scott Billington, who followed suit on *Simply Grand*.

Billington pairs Thomas with various piano accompanists — among them Randy Newman, Dr. John, Tom McDermott, Norah Jones and Ellis Marsalis. Their personalities set the direction, but the relatively spare backing gives Thomas room to inhabit the dramatic trepidation of "Overrated" (with Davell Crawford) and the dance of hope and loss in the Burt Bacharach-penned "What Can I Do" (with David Torkanowsky). She's similarly given free reign to employ all the textures she can

summon in her voice, along with dynamic modulations that sometimes underscore the lyric and other times give lie to the words.

In fact, it's hard to recall when Thomas has shown more resourcefulness as a singer. No emotion or attitude sounds rote here, even when she's on familiar ground. The Caribbean flavor of John Fogerty's spiritual "River Is Waiting" helps Thomas find a fresh note of joy in the message, and she sings David Egan's "Underground Stream" with a low, controlled conviction in the presence of the unseen.

But as much as she exercises her full range of vocal possibilities, her performances are unified by the knowledge that comes from life and musical experience. She sings the blues as if she's lived with them and knows enough to be amused by them at times. She knows the cost of lost love, and she can signal that sometimes her songs tell stories which aren't necessarily *her* stories. On "Be You," she enjoys the song as simply a song, having fun with Dr. John and the clever expressions of love he wrote with Doc Pomus. "I'll be your every kind of money/When you're down to your last dime," she sings.

By embracing the songs as songs, Thomas moves closer to being an "entertainer," but she also moves toward a more interesting artistic stance. Rightly or wrongly, people have heard her expressions of pain, spirit and triumph as chapters of her life story set to music. Perhaps it's the degree to which she has embraced the blues — framing herself as a genre singer — or maybe it's the song choices, but there's little temptation to hear *After The Rain* or *Simply Grand* as pages from her diary.

This deepens her artistry, because she's not merely reliving old emotions; she's finding her connections to songs, empathizing with the person whose thoughts are presented in the lyric. Obviously, she and Billington chose songs that didn't require her to inhabit completely foreign personas, but as a jazz vocalist on "This Bitter Earth," she's ruminative and musically curious, exploring the songs ideas and melodic possibilities in a way that is very different than what you'd expect from "the Soul Queen of New Orleans."

I love this Thomas, more than the soap-operatic Thomas, and more than the gospel Thomas who sings Mahalia Jackson tributes at Jazz Fest. I respect both, but when she brings the spirituality, drama, passion, wisdom, theatricality, and musicality that she has lived and learned over the years to her own music, the results are beautiful and complex. She's honest, if she's not exactly keeping it real, and while her personality unifies her set — the entertainer's trick — she doesn't rely on it solely. She's still aware of her audience, and the themes don't stray too far from those she has sung before, but the album isn't tailored to her audience. *Simply Grand* reflects where Thomas is now, without being autobiographical. And in that way, she's an entertainer in the best sense of the word.   — ALEX RAWLS

WILLIE NELSON & WYNTON MARSALIS

Two Men With The Blues

(Blue Note)

THIS COLLABORATION is less surprising than it might seem. For decades, Willie Nelson has developed a parallel career collaborating in the studio and onstage; some of the projects are personal in nature, while others, like this one, clearly are conceived to maintain and expand his already-broad appeal. A jazz collaboration is hardly a reach. Growing up in Abbott, Texas, Nelson absorbed jazz from the radio with the same fervor he did Leon Payne or Bob Wills. Jazz sensibilities crept into some of his earliest recordings. That remained apparent in 1970, before the world beyond Nashville and Texas knew he existed, when Miles Davis named an instrumental for him.

Trumpet virtuoso Wynton Marsalis' participation is more significant. Teaming with a musician perceived by much of the world as "country" — even one as transcendent as Willie — holds a bit of irony. While singing Nelson's praises to the media as a senior creative consultant for Ken Burns' dilettantish 2001 PBS documentary *Jazz*, the classically-trained Marsalis made condescending, arbitrary remarks about white jazz musicians that angered and offended many of both races. Granted, no one denies Marsalis' jazz skills; yet his own music has drawn flak for accentuating older styles (Dixieland, swing, bebop and blues) and denying the past 40-plus years of changes in jazz.

Those earlier eras provide the context on this live album, recorded at New York City's Lincoln Center over two nights in January 2007. Nelson and his longtime harmonica player Mickey Raphael teamed with Marsalis and a quartet of younger jazz players. While Nelson's jazz-like vocal phrasing fits the ensemble hand-in-glove, the repertoire is largely predictable; they begin with Jimmy Reed's "Bright Lights, Big City" and the inevitable reprise of Nelson's "Night Life," replete with blues, jazz, and ample room to improvise. Here, Willie throws in a brief but astringent guitar break before Raphael takes over. Singers typically shout the frenetic 1940s Louis Jordan R&B chestnut "Caldonia"; Nelson simply adapts it to his own quirky vocal phrasing.

The reprises of "Stardust" and "Basin Street Blues," jazz standards long a part of Nelson's repertoire, were inevitable. Nonetheless, on "Stardust," Marsalis and his band, whether treading old ground or not, create a rewarding collaboration with their work between Willie's bookended vocals. It's virtually impossible to screw up "Basin Street," and they don't. "Georgia On My Mind" is muscular and totally focused, pianist Dan Nimmer providing diamond-hard accompaniment throughout. The biggest disappointment is "Rainy Day Blues," the B-side to Willie's 1960 Houston recording of "Night Life"; Marsalis and company could have exploited its nuanced harmonic complexity, but instead, it's recast as a mere shuffle.

Clarence Williams' "My Bucket's Got A Hole In It," a song identified with both Hank Williams and Louis Armstrong, rides jauntily atop drummer Ali Jackson's crisp Crescent City rhythms. The most interesting aspect of "Bucket" and the next number, the blues classic "Ain't Nobody's Business," is that Willie and Marsalis swap vocals. Try as he might, Marsalis is simply too stiff and ill-at-ease to pull off what Armstrong did as a matter of routine. The conclusion, a churning take on Merle Travis' "That's All," becomes a free-for-all as everyone throws in choruses; saxophonist Walter Blanding wails away like King Curtis behind the Coasters.

It's no surprise that *Two Men With The Blues* spawned a veritable flood of media coverage. Still, it brings forth nothing new or revolutionary, nor was it meant to. Armstrong and his pianist wife Lillian backed Jimmie Rodgers on "Blue Yodel # 9" in 1930; Stan Kenton's bombastic west coast jazz orchestra recorded a 1962 album with Tex Ritter. This is merely the latest in the continuum.

— RICH KIENZLE

RAY LAMONTAGNE
Gossip In The Grain
(RCA)

SOMETIME in the past few years, Ray LaMontagne, a soulful, depressive, shaggy dog of a folk singer, became a mainstream pop star complete with a Top-40 album, gigs at Radio City Music Hall, and a female fan base prone to panty-throwing.

In other words, LaMontagne has, for reasons that continue to bewilder, become the designated broody male singer-songwriter of choice for people who don't usually like broody male singer-songwriters. He seems to appeal equally to pop fans (thanks in small part to Kelly Clarkson's actually-pretty-super cover of his famed "Shelter"), modern rock fans, and jam-band fans otherwise fond of Jack Johnson and Dave Matthews.

LaMontagne's music isn't particularly accessible, nor is his onstage persona particularly compelling: Painfully awkward, shy to the point of semi-consciousness, he has been known to play concerts in the dark. He may be the least fun person ever in the history of folk singing. And this includes Nick Drake.

Gossip In The Grain, his third album, won't do much to alter anyone's perceptions of LaMontagne one way or the other. His first offering with a full band (and his third collaboration with producer Ethan Johns), the disc differs only slightly from its predecessors. It doesn't rock, exactly, but it has a less claustrophobic feel than LaMontagne's earnest, airless past works, while leaving his standard sonic palette — the shivery ballads, the slow-burning mid-tempo numbers — pretty much intact.

LaMontagne is an old-school crooner in the fashion of Otis Redding or even Ray Charles, with a remarkable voice made for bluesier stuff than this. His lyrics have a mustiness to them that must be intentional; no one comes up with this many farming metaphors by accident. Songs can be divided into two categories:

A) I'm Knocking at Your Back Door, Mama; and

B) Mama, Where'd You Go?

Gossip In The Grain suggests some weird mixture of oft-cited influences such as Van Morrison, The Band, and, on its nominally rollicking tracks (like the finger-picking, porch-stomping "Hey Me, Hey Mama"), the Felice Brothers impersonating The Band. If Ryan Adams spent too much time with the *Cold Mountain* soundtrack and then made an album about it, this is what would happen.

The variations from LaMontagne's usual gently-strummed guitar ballads are few: The dark, unaccountably menacing "Henry Nearly Killed Me (It's A Shame)" is a riot of handclaps and harmonicas; the '60s psychedelic pop-inspired "Meg White" is intended as a (light-hearted?) homage to the White Stripes drummer, perhaps the only contemporary artist as solemn-faced as he. ("Some day I'd like to take a walk with you," he sings, "maybe ride our bikes down by the seaside.") Most of the tracks hew closely to the sort of bluesy, achy slow songs LaMontagne does well, and often. The record-opening "Let It Be Me" recalls the superior "Shelter"; "A Falling Through" is a stripped-down and whispery duet with Leona Naess.

It's a trick of LaMontagne's voice, of his amazing instrument and its excessive grav-ity, that his albums sound deeper and weightier than they actually are. On first listen, *Gossip In The Grain* is throaty and soulful and mysterious, possessing multitudes. The more you hear it, the less substantive it feels, as if the whole enterprise was imbued with a heft its individual songs don't always deserve. There's ultimately nothing that sticks — no memorable choruses, no meaty hooks, no thought-provoking lyrics, just a succession of amorphous songs that don't quite manage to make their point before wandering off.

LaMontagne might one day become a songwriter to be reckoned with, once he learns to hitch his formidable voice to something concrete. But three albums in, this may be all there is: a formless batch of woeful phrases wrapped around scraggly almost-choruses, wisps of air where the songs should be.

— ALLISON STEWART

RY COODER
I, Flathead
(Nonesuch)

THE WORST thing you can do with *I, Flathead* is treat it with too much respect. You can think about how Ry Cooder turned down a chance to play with the Rolling Stones, how he unearthed the Buena Vista Social Club, how he's fluent on more stringed instruments playing more musical styles than most anyone alive, and how he's culminating his California Trilogy — his third concept album in four years — not only with these fourteen new, all-original tunes, but, for those who buy the deluxe edition, a 95-page novella. You can try to parse all the real or imagined allegories, koans, and back-to-future commentaries involved in a project with a title meant to invoke Isaac

Asimov's *I, Robot*; an album that includes an impersonation of Richard Nixon as narrator of a song titled "Flathead One More Time"; an opus that features among its main characters a space alien named Shakey who races cars out on the salt flats in the early 1960s with a musician named Kash Buk (who, together with his band, the Klowns, purportedly wrote all the songs for *I, Flathead*).

Or you can let it groove. Pop it in your player and let your body take the first swipe at culling the cockamamie goofs from the pathways to wisdom. Because that's the fun part.

Cooder has always been about both sides of the Paradise and Lunch equation. When I was a teenager, one of my favorite songs on his eponymous 1970 debut was his yawling vocal on "One Meatball." A few years later, living in a Seattle house full of transplanted Haight Asbury hippies, I'd watch them get stoned and trip out to a Ry record (*Paradise And Lunch*, in fact) nearly as often as they would with the Stones and the Dead. More than 30 years later, he's still serving up the musical equivalent of daffy duck paté. On this album's opening track, "Drive Like I Never Been Hurt," Kash Buk goes into full Jimmy Swaggart mode testifying about car parts and other lingo cribbed from *Popular Mechanics*, while mariachi horns sway in the background. The prettiest ditty on the disc by a mile is titled "My Dwarf Is Getting Tired," a pristine country-swing ballad about Disneyland usurping the circus.

Cooder fans will be ecstatic to know he breaks out the slide guitar to send up the McCarthy blacklisting era for "Pink-O Boogie," a swamp-rocker reminiscent of Little Feat. "Steel Guitar Heaven" creates space for shout-outs to some of Cooder's mentors, along with imparting the revelation that God has deco-

rated the place in green and gold shag carpeting and red naugahyde. And "Spayed Kooley" melds two of Cooder's pet pleasures: It's a western-swing tune that bowdlerizes the name of bandleader (and wife killer) Spade Cooley, and it's about a dog who will rip you to shreds if you don't sing on key or properly recite the Pledge of Allegiance. (You may recall that the second edition of Cooder's trilogy, 2007's *My Name Is Buddy*, was narrated by a cat, a mouse and a toad.)

What I liked about that "One Meatball" vocal way back when was that Cooder knew he couldn't sing southern country blues as authentically as Josh White (who was blacklisted during the McCarthy era, by the way), but he didn't want to sound like some earnest white poseur either, so he hammed it up. His Kash Buk does the same thing, going overboard on the Man in Black to avoid pretension while walking the line on the slap-rhythm of a track titled "Johnny Cash." But that's Cooder's natural voice imploring a cheerleader to "pull up your dress and kick off your shoes" while mainlining bottleneck riffs on the Stonesy "Ridin' With The Blues." He saves the nuance for his dissolute wino chatting up a lady on the talk-sung "Can I Smoke In Here?", masterfully coordinating the midpoint between creepy stalker and sympathetically hard-luck drifter.

Don't ask me how the numerous socio-historical references in *I, Flathead* all add up. I haven't grooved to it enough yet. Besides, if I'm seriously inclined to get to the bottom of something, I'll crack open *The Dark Side*, journalist Jane Mayer's new tome on American torture. I suspect Ry Cooder wouldn't have it any other way.

— BRITT ROBSON